HELEN OXENBURY

a life in illustration

LEONARD S. MARCUS

CANDLEWICK PRESS

First U.S. edition 2019

Library of Congress Catalog Card Number 2018961623
ISBN 978-0-7636-9258-2

19 20 21 22 23 24 CCP 10 9 8 7 6 5 4 3 2 1

Printed in Shenzhen, Guangdong, China

This book was typeset in Diotima.

Candlewick Press
99 Dover Street
Somerville, Massachusetts 02144

visit us at www.candlewick.com

FOR MY GRANDCHILDREN

H. O.

FOR DAVID BRION DAVIS
INSPIRED TEACHER

*"To be yourself in a world that is constantly
trying to make you something else
is the greatest accomplishment."*

Emerson

———————————

L. S. M.

Table of Contents

*"It is impossible to be too much
on the side of the child."*

Helen Oxenbury

———————————

HELEN OXENBURY

the interview

LEONARD S. MARCUS

I FIRST *met Helen Oxenbury in 1989, on a gray November morning in New York. She had arrived from London the previous afternoon, and our 10 a.m. interview was to be her first appointment on a crowded eight-city American promotional tour. I wrote for a magazine read by parents like the ones who bought her wise and superbly drawn picture books. Parents chose the books for their toddlers and preschool children and were often surprised to find how much they enjoyed the books too. Helen Oxenbury, it seemed, knew young children and their parents equally well: she understood how hard it was to be a new mom or dad and how impossibly hard it must be, at times, to be a baby — a brand-new person in the world. What was more, she had a gift for crafting words and pictures that brought adult and child closer together. How did she know her readers so well? As I waited in the featureless white room that her publisher had set aside for our interview, I wondered what this well-loved artist with not just one but five new books on offer that fall would have to say.*

I had been writing about children's books by then for a good fifteen years — both as a journalist and as a biographer and historian — and had come to regard Helen Oxenbury as one of the genre's indispensable figures. She had published an extraordinary body of work, a long shelf of knowing, smart, and deeply affectionate illustrated books that gave young children a true-to-life picture of their world. I knew from my historical travels that books as deceptively simple as Helen Oxenbury's were apt to be underappreciated by some. I also knew that real simplicity in art was almost never easily come by and that wholly satisfying baby and toddler books like hers were exceedingly rare.

At 10 a.m. the conference room door swung open and in walked a Macmillan publicist followed by Helen Oxenbury, looking relaxed, I thought, after her long flight. She smiled the warm smile I recognized from her official photo.

"You must be tired," I said.

"Just a bit," she replied, taking the measure of her words as we sat down opposite each other, a tape recorder between us.

"Oh, but don't worry about that," she said, her voice brightening into a burst of friendly reassurance.

I pressed the on button, and for the next two hours we spoke about many things.

We talked about Helen's earliest memories of books and about the experience of growing up in wartime Britain. ("I thoroughly enjoyed the war," she declared with mischief in her voice. "You see, I didn't really know what was going on.") She described the jolt and rush of leaving the east of England for London as a twenty-year-old art student. (No, it had not been all glamour and glory: "London seemed like another country, and I was very, very lonely for the first year.") We discussed her uncompromising commitment to her art, her marriage to author and artist John Burningham, the challenges of being

a working mother, and the path by which her experiences in that hugely important area of her life had come to serve her well as material. We talked about the five new books whose release she had come to the United States to celebrate.

Four of those five books represented the American launch of the Tom and Pippo series: large-format first storybooks about a doughty toddler, Tom, and the cloth monkey who is his trusted companion, comic foil, and springboard to imagining himself as the bigger, wiser, more responsible half in a parent-child relationship.

Helen's fifth new fall book, a collaboration with the writer Michael Rosen, was called We're Going on a Bear Hunt and marked a notable departure for her on a number of counts. For one thing, it was a book of unusually large format by both her own and industry standards. For another, it was as much about landscape as it was about people. There was also something strikingly original about the book's overall look and design. From the moment I had opened a review copy earlier that fall, I had known the book was special. For once, the oxymoronic marketing catchphrase "instant classic" seemed no more or less than the fact of the matter.

That morning I had packed a copy of Beatrix Potter's The Tale of Peter Rabbit, curious to know what Helen Oxenbury might have to say about it. Her eyes lit up as I placed the little book before her, and, scanning its pages, she paused

over the illustration of Peter about to lose his blue jacket as he slips under the fence into Mr. McGregor's garden. I asked her what made the book so memorable.

"Things happen," she said, "that involve all the emotions. It starts off with a safe family. Then Peter does the very thing he's been told not to do. There's a slight tension and fear, the feeling that something is looming. He's seen by Mr. McGregor the gardener, and then there is the great chase, and . . . It's a very good adventure story."

"Beatrix Potter metes out justice in the end," I pointed out, "making Peter pay with a bellyache for his wild adventure, but it is not this or any lesson that readers are left with."

"That's right," said Helen, closing the book. "It's just good natural naughtiness" — a clear-eyed glimpse, as in her own stories and illustrations, not of things as they should be but rather of things as they are.

Then it was time for the next event in Helen's American book tour — a telephone interview with a reporter from Salt Lake City. Not all children's book people, I had long since discovered, were quite as lovable as their creations. But as we said our goodbyes, it struck me that the artist I had just met was very much the person I had already encountered in the pages of her books: the wry and perceptive observer of people, places, and things; the consummate professional; the champion of children; and — considering the timing of our morning get-together — the generous good sport.

From We're Going on a Bear Hunt, *Walker, 1989*

Later, as I played back the tape, I picked up on a paradox that had presented itself in our conversation: Helen's books had the mark of perfection about them. Yet their theme, so often, was our human need to accept one another in all our imperfection, parent and child alike. As an artist, Helen had said, she herself found it hard to feel satisfied with her work, especially once it was published. Yet, as though to balance out this self-critical impulse, she took great pride in the fact that her art was constantly evolving.

"I've changed quite a lot," she said. "We're Going on a Bear Hunt is quite a bit different from the work I was doing even three years ago."

When I asked Helen what might be next, she replied, "I have a feeling that I want my drawings to be much freer now."

As she said this, she paused to consider just how that might feel.

At Home in London

Sometimes, when she is at home in London, Helen Oxenbury begins her working day at a favorite neighborhood coffeehouse. The work she does there does not look much like work.

She starts by selecting a small table and ordering a large coffee. No papers or pencils come out onto the table. Next, Myles, her commanding Jack Russell, takes his place on the chair next to hers. He knows the routine and is already on the alert when a passerby or customer across the room suddenly catches the artist's attention. It is then that the day's work begins.

"I start to wonder," Helen has said of what happens next, "what this person does for a living. What's the relationship between those two? Is that her husband or lover? Is that his wife or girlfriend? It's a kind of comedy, totally based on appearance and filed away for characters to come."

An old friend who has watched Helen watching people in this way over the years has observed the exact moment when she knows she has seen enough. A change, he suggests, will sweep across her face as, for just an instant, both her eyes close — *click!* — like an old-fashioned camera shutter. "Done and done," as another old friend of Helen's, with a fondness for an antique

turn of phrase, would say. Time perhaps for Helen to head to her studio.

The Territory of Childhood

In the art of Helen Oxenbury, seeing is a way of knowing, and drawing a form of felt experience. In the great variety of books she has illustrated over nearly fifty years, Helen has mapped out the territory of childhood in drawings that combine the intimacy of a family snapshot with the formal mastery of a searching and rigorous art. A perfectionist with a restless dislike of repeating herself, she has been a pioneer in children's literature, creating books of compelling interest to babies, toddlers, and (wisely) their parents and, in Britain, opening the once all-white world of the picture book to children of color. She has given readers fresh reinterpretations of time-honored classics and added classic picture books of her own that build freely on the dynamic tradition set by Randolph Caldecott, Beatrix Potter, and Edward Ardizzone. It is remarkable to realize that all this has gone on, for decades, in the same household where another of the world's most original picture book artists, Helen's husband, John Burningham, has also been hard at work.

Helen (left) and her brother, John, in Felixstowe, c. 1940

The Ardent Youngster

Helen, it seems, was always going to be some sort of artist. Born in 1938 in Ipswich, in the county of Suffolk in the east of England, she suffered from asthma as a young child, a condition that periodically left her bedridden. Drawing became a favorite distraction and a lifeline. No great reader as a child, she made do with whatever books she had at hand. The first picture book she recalls with pleasure was a very brash photo album of the American film sensation Shirley Temple. It made no difference that she had not seen any of the charismatic child star's sun-splashed films. For a time, Helen dreamed of becoming a tap dancer but had to settle for ballet lessons. Enid Blyton's Famous Five novels became firm favorites, while other stories were read aloud by Helen's mother, Muriel, whose special feeling for Lewis Carroll's Alice books left an impression with lasting consequences. It hardly mattered that books in general were in short supply. When the ardent youngster reached the end of a particularly absorbing Blyton novel, she simply turned back to page one and read it again.

Children's books with full-color art were a scarce commodity in Britain generally. Publishers treated color as hoarded treasure, to be dispensed at rare intervals between long expanses of type and black-line drawings or silhouettes. Helen came to love the dramatic reveal of the occasional full-color plate in the *Blackie's Children's Annuals* her mother passed on to her, and to appreciate the impact of color when used sparingly. Books, she learned early on, were not in any case objects to hoard or feel precious about. Nearly all the children's books in the Oxenbury household were on loan from the local library.

The Look of Things

Helen's father, Bernard Oxenbury, was an architect who had carved out a professional niche as an author of government-sponsored regional land use plans. The look of things and visual awareness mattered deeply to him. In the 1950s he was among the first to judge the best-kept village competition, aimed at beautifying communities and bolstering civic pride via a proliferation of flower boxes and well-trimmed lawns. At home he collected oil paintings and dabbled in marquetry and painting in watercolors, once producing for Helen and her brother a beguiling drawing of a "community of elves living in the roots of a tree which overhung a river." Other times he entertained them by painting pictures of their toys. Had he dreamed of becoming an illustrator? His daughter would later wonder about this. In any event, he encouraged her first artistic efforts and sent her drawings off to competitions in which Helen sometimes took the prize.

By the age of six, Helen had found that she enjoyed drawing people best of all. She would wait for a family member to become absorbed in some activity — her grandfather sitting by the radio for hours listening to a cricket match suited her needs perfectly —

A SAD MISHAP!

then she would take out her art supplies and settle down to work.

Ipswich's deepwater harbor and railway goods yards made the town a target for German aerial bombardment throughout the war. The Oxenburys had built an underground bomb shelter in their garden into which they descended whenever the warning siren sounded. Neighbors would sometimes join them to await the all-clear over a cup of tea. The shelter was fitted with bunk beds, but young Helen resisted sleep, not so much out of fear

Above: A Sad Mishap! — a drawing by Helen's father, Bernard, taken from his autograph book
Facing page: Helen's childhood drawing of her grandpa, c. 1946

MY GRANDPA

HGO:

as from the sheer drama of being there. The war was apt to seem more unreal than not to a well-cared-for young child living outside London. One incident finally brought home the war's horrific nature for a child's comprehension: the crash-landing of a German bomber, more or less intact, on an Ipswich bridge. Found dead in the cockpit beside the dead pilot was the pilot's dog.

Wartime rationing took an emotional toll, especially on Muriel, "queuing up for a tiny bit of fish, which she'd give to us children, and half a pound of butter for the week." Winters were already cold and harsh, and for Helen the image of her mother rising early each morning to lay a new fire in the open hearth packed the force of a haunting cautionary tale. Years later she would wonder aloud what sort of career Muriel, an outgoing woman who loved to entertain, meet people, and dance, might have pursued had she only been given the chance. Helen resolved to find some way not to share that fate. Long before she left Suffolk she would decide that art might be the answer.

A Spirited Girl

Around the time Helen turned eight, the Oxenburys, seeking relief for their daughter's chronic asthma, moved twelve miles southeast

Helen (left), her brother, John (right), and their grandpa (middle), seen here with his pipe as captured in Helen's childhood drawing on page 31, c. 1948

from Ipswich to the seaside resort of Felixstowe. The plan worked so well that Helen soon discovered a whole new side to herself. She became a competitive tennis player who enjoyed sports, taking off with friends on ambitious bike rides past the ghostly stone fortifications built along the shore during Napoleonic times, and disappearing on messy walks through the nearby mudflats.

During the long, damp Suffolk winters, holidaymakers migrated elsewhere, the shops that catered to them were closed, and young people like Helen had little to do besides dream of the world that lay beyond Suffolk. After school, there were the radio serials about Special Agent Dick Barton to distract her, and film matinees on weekends. A single ticket entitled the movie-goer to watch unlimited showings of a double feature repeated throughout the day; Helen's favorites were always Hollywood musicals such as *An American in Paris* and *Singin' in the Rain*.

Helen playing tennis as a teenager, c. 1954

Glamorous Images

To a romantic teenager with glamorous images of far-off America in her head, Bentwaters, the air base that the RAF had handed over to the American 81st Fighter Wing after the war, became a focus of endless speculation. At the age of fourteen or fifteen, Helen and her friends dressed up like the American airmen's wives in white ankle socks and men's white shirts worn untucked. Completing the spectacle, they put up their hair in curlers wrapped in colorful scarves. The object was to get invited to a base dance. The Americans seemed, however, to be under strict orders not to mix with the local population. In any case, the friends' elaborate machinations got them nowhere. As Helen attended to her school studies, she considered her prospects for a life beyond Felixstowe.

"Drawing," she later recalled, "was one of the few things I had always been good at in school." With her father's blessing, Helen enrolled in the Ipswich School of Art, where she received a rigorous introduction to sculpting, architecture, still life, and life drawing that she thoroughly enjoyed. One favorite instructor made a lasting impression through the bracing sarcasm of his tough-minded critiques, an uncompromising approach that fueled Helen's own perfectionism. "You jolly well sat down and you drew the human body, and if it wasn't right then you'd just start again."

Suffolk folk referred with pride to John Constable, the great Romantic landscape painter, as one of their own, and recalled that film actor John Mills had spent part of his boyhood in Suffolk, and that Eric Arthur Blair had taken his pen name — George Orwell — from the River Orwell, which flowed through Suffolk near his parents' home. More often, however, people spoke disparagingly of a portion of England that "wasn't on the way through to anywhere," as Helen herself would later observe. Still, she would retain a lifelong love of the region and return to it often for days or weeks at a time. But it was hardly the place for a young artist who was ready to burnish her craft.

The wide-ranging Ipswich curriculum was designed to prepare the way for more advanced training elsewhere. To Helen, there was "only one place to specialize in anything" — London.

"Felixstowe can make it"
Exhibition, 1947.

DRAWINGS &c:.

GILLIAN OXENBURY.

1st PRIZE.

Above: The certificate from the "Felixstowe can make it" exhibition where Helen —
then known by her middle name, Gillian — won first prize, aged 9
Facing page: Helen at art college, c. 1958
Next page: From Alice's Adventures in Wonderland, Walker, 1999

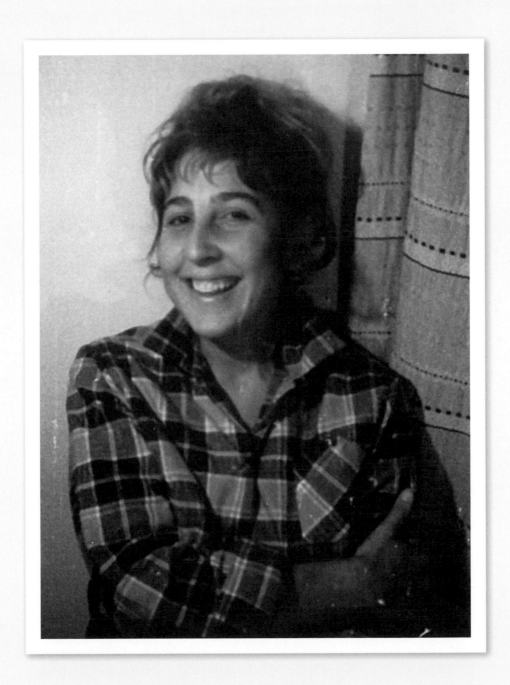

"Now, I'll manage better this time,"
she said to herself, and began by
taking the little golden key, and
unlocking the door that led
into the garden.

---

from Lewis Carroll's

Alice's Adventures in Wonderland *(1865)*

1957–1962

A Study in Contrasts
Comedy
Adventure
Turning Points

A Study in Contrasts

The caliber of the students at London's Central School of Art and Design, known originally as the Central School of Art and Crafts, where Helen enrolled in the theater arts department from 1957 to 1959, was high. Her classmates included Sally Jacobs, soon to be one of Britain's most celebrated stage designers through her work for the Royal Shakespeare Company; Peter Brook; and others.

Students rarely ventured outside their own department, even socially. So it was by more or less a great stroke of luck that a mutual friend happened to introduce Helen to a graphic design and illustration student in the year above her by the name of John Burningham.

In many respects, Helen and John were a study in contrasts. He was by turns taciturn and boisterous, with a rich stage baritone, an impish knack for mimicry, and an explosive laugh. She was a bit shy, though her sly wit easily found its mark in an offhand comment grounded in keen observation, especially of people. He seemed at home amid chaotic surroundings, a messy clutter of possibilities. She preferred classical order and clarity. He had a wide-ranging curiosity about the history of illustration and of art in general. She had spent far less time immersing herself in the art of the past. Happily for

Previous pages: Helen at her studio, c. 1968
Facing page: Helen and John Burningham while at London's Central School of Art together, c. 1958

the relationship that became their marriage, she thought him the better artist and he thought the same about her.

Comedy

For Helen, London on a student stipend was a tight fit. No evenings out for her to catch the latest John Osborne or Harold Pinter production, although both playwrights had major new works in the West End during her college years. She did manage to acquire a stylish duffel coat for herself and a ticket to the original London cast production of *West Side Story*, the raw dynamism of which thrilled her. The jazz of Oscar Peterson and Erroll Garner came into her room via a student record player; she replayed the latter's milestone *Concert by the Sea* again and again, as she had once reread Enid Blyton. With what little money she had left over, Helen sought out comedy wherever it was to be found. At the Fortune Theatre, for instance, the Oxford-bred duo who called themselves Flanders

44

and Swann performed songs and dialogues by turns archly satirical and unapologetically silly. Among the pair's crowd-pleasers was the rousing "Hippopotamus Song" — "Mud, mud, glorious mud / Nothing quite like it for cooling the blood" — innocent fun for a generation for whom fun, not all that long ago, had been in nearly as short supply as bananas and bread.

Adventure

On graduating from the Central School of Art and Design, Helen joined the Colchester Repertory Theatre as an assistant designer, while John left for Israel, where he had previously performed a portion of his alternative military service as a conscientious objector, and where he now had a job building puppets for an animated film by Yoram Gross based on Thomas Mann's *Joseph and His Brothers.* John shuttled back and forth between what seemed like two worlds. During one long absence from England, he sent Helen a plane ticket. When she arrived in Israel, however, it was only to learn that he intended to return to Britain in a matter of weeks.

"Do you want to come back with me?" John asked her, rather sheepishly, one imagines.

"Well, I'm staying on" was the answer.

Helen's set design for Billy Liar *at Habima, Israel's national theater, c. 1960*

Helen, who had not ventured abroad previously, recalled: "I wasn't going to have gone all that way just to turn around and go back."

Determined to have *some* sort of adventure, Helen found work as an au pair and a tutor of conversational English before landing a more satisfying job at Habima, Israel's national theater, in Tel Aviv. The handsome new performance center resounded with the boisterous, resonant voices of transplanted Russian Jewish actors, artists, and technicians and hummed with the idealism and energy of the gleaming white modernist desert city. A stupendously ambitious cultural experiment was unfolding before her eyes, and Helen was thrilled to be a part of it. Starting out as a scenic painter, she advanced to set designer and came fully into her own when the company mounted a production of *Billy Liar*, a contemporary comedy that took place in an English north-country house.

Now it was John's turn to visit Helen, blowing into Tel Aviv on the Lambretta scooter he had purchased after seeing William Wyler's *Roman Holiday*. Rejoining Helen in Israel, he now invited her in effect to play Audrey Hepburn to his Gregory Peck, and together they took off on weekend adventures, threading south through the Negev Desert to Eilat, then just a cluster of makeshift guard posts and fishermen's huts; and north to Caesarea, where they walked among the Roman ruins.

Helen and John riding through the Negev Desert on a weekend adventure, c. 1960

Turning Points

The early 1960s was to be a time of personal and professional turning points for both John and Helen. After briefly considering remaining permanently in Israel, Helen returned to England in 1962, where she found work first at ABC (Associated British Corporation) Television, and then at Shepperton Studios, in Surrey, where Judy Garland was shooting *I Could Go On Singing*. John, having set up shop as a graphic artist in a dingy Soho basement, scored his first major success as a poster designer for London Transport.

John also had an unpublished children's book in his portfolio. With that in mind, a friend introduced him to Tom Maschler, an up-and-coming editor at the publishing house of Jonathan Cape. Maschler fell under the spell of the artist's raffish drawings. *Borka: The Adventures of a Goose with No Feathers* was published by Cape in 1963, attracted eight foreign editions, and won the year's Kate Greenaway Medal. Suddenly, the future looked bright — bright enough for John and Helen to marry and move to Hampstead, London.

A young Helen at art college

1960s

A Way to Proceed

Hampstead would gradually gentrify all around them, but in Helen and John's first years it remained, if hardly bohemian, a heady enclave of artists, writers, and intellectuals.

John le Carré and Alfred Brendel lived in the neighborhood; so did Sir Kenneth Clark and Ian Fleming. John would publish two picture books in 1965 and one or more in nearly every year thereafter for decades to come. But with the birth of their first child, Lucy, in 1965, Helen's future seemed a good deal more tentative.

It was clear to her that the theater career she had trained for was now out of the question. As she mulled over her professional options, first one idea came to mind, then another, both involving one of their closest mutual friends.

The couple had met Polish-born artist-designer Jan Pieńkowski when John and Pieńkowski were contributing illustrators for the weekly *Time and Tide*. Pieńkowski had a quick wit, hip contemporary design sense, and a good head for business.

Having come to live in Britain after the war as a seven-year-old, he read English and classics at King's College, Cambridge, then began illustrating children's books and launched Gallery Five, a greeting card company with a shop in London's West End that caused a sensation.

Previous pages: Helen with her daughter Lucy (left) and her son, Bill (right), c. 1968

The typical greeting card of the time was a dreary affair featuring a rose and a little bit of gold trim. Pieńkowski thought of a card as affordable art to be created and then shared by the purchaser with friends and family. Gallery Five designs were not for traditionalists, but for younger Britons who were keen on putting the gray years of rationing behind them; they signaled nothing less than a generational changing of the guard.

When Pieńkowski invited his artist friends to contribute illustrations, Helen was among those who said yes. She saw in the offer a way to proceed creatively, at least in the short run. A card was a one-off project that could be completed at the kitchen table with a baby on one's lap. A card design presented the chance — a small chance, anyway — to draw the people she observed and to comment on, among other things, what it was really like to be a modern mother.

It was a small step from there to realizing that a collection of such drawings, if unified by a common theme or game-like

structure, could come together as a picture book. Pieńkowski and John both urged her to give it a whirl. The first book Helen created in this way was a counting book called *Numbers of Things*, with a merry pyramid of six — count them! — acrobats featured on the cover. The drawings, with their stylish arrangements of nine birds on one page and twenty balloons on another, were powered by a rigorously fugue-like sense of composition and by the deadpan humor of characters with slightly flustered looks on their faces, as though pleasantly surprised to have wandered into the picture.

It seemed only wise for Helen to launch her book career at a publisher other than the one where John had already established

Above: Vegetable Garden, *Gallery Five, 1980*
Facing page: When Jan Pieńkowski (off-camera) came to Helen's studio for work sessions, he often brought along his dog Beauty — a major distraction, as seen here, c. 1972.

Numbers of Things
Helen Oxenbury

himself. She found a warm reception at Heinemann, which brought out *Numbers of Things* in 1967. For the following year, her editor gave her free rein to choose any story she wished to illustrate. Helen selected a traditional Russian tale, *The Great Big Enormous Turnip*, as retold by Alexei Tolstoy.

2
two
cars

4
four
mice

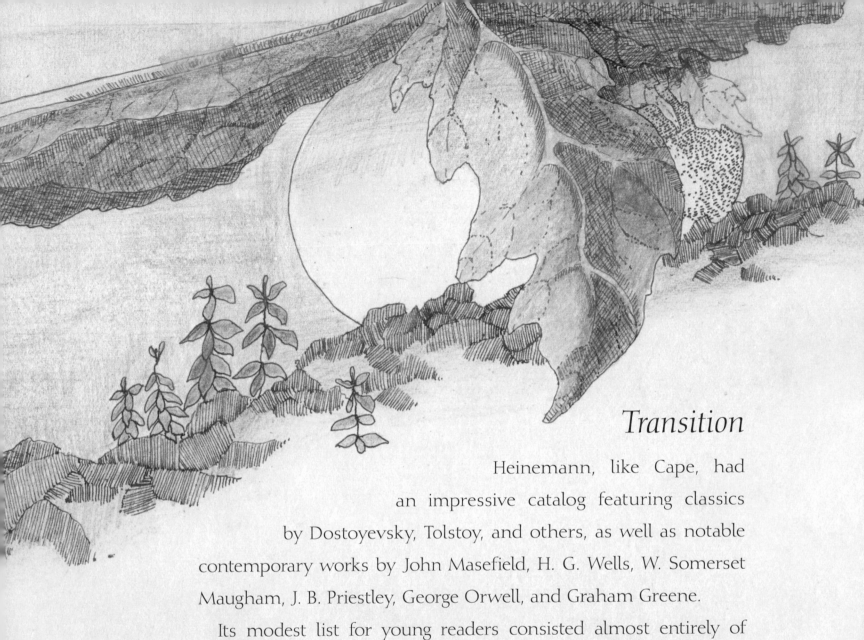

Transition

Heinemann, like Cape, had
an impressive catalog featuring classics
by Dostoyevsky, Tolstoy, and others, as well as notable
contemporary works by John Masefield, H. G. Wells, W. Somerset
Maugham, J. B. Priestley, George Orwell, and Graham Greene.

Its modest list for young readers consisted almost entirely of
the occasional juvenile title produced by a Heinemann author on a
busman's holiday. A staff of one, with no budget for advertising,
oversaw what was obviously regarded as a secondary branch of
the business.

From The Great Big Enormous Turnip, *Heinemann, 1968*

Heinemann was in fact typical of postwar British publishers in this regard. Notwithstanding England's glorious legacy of children's literature classics, contemporary British firms were only just awakening to the need for a well-structured and systematic approach to juvenile publishing. Helen, like John Burningham, would have to weather the gyrations of an old-fashioned industry in transition.

All in all, however, the couple's timing was fortunate. Public libraries in Britain had funding for the purchase of children's books, and publishers began to build their lists accordingly, in the knowledge that a reliable market awaited any book of quality on which they were willing to take a chance.

Of far greater import for publishers and the authors themselves, as postwar prosperity spread across Europe and to portions of Asia, was the unprecedented international market for children's books that was starting to coalesce. In 1964 the Bologna Children's Book Fair was created as an annual gathering for publishers to buy and sell foreign rights and discuss the future of their industry. The handful of publishers who made the trip in the early years were ardent internationalists who believed that sharing the best children's books with young people across national borders could help the world become a more peaceful place.

Global Stars

Publishers meeting in Bologna found a clever way to put their idealism to work while also saving themselves some money. They realized that if they banded together in ad hoc partnerships with houses from other noncompeting national markets, they could lower their color printing costs by taking advantage of economies of scale.

The more partners who participated in an international "co-edition," the more copies could be printed in a single press run, thus bringing down the cost per copy for all.

The vastly expanded potential audience for picture books created through these collaborative arrangements set the stage for the emergence of the field's first global stars. Early members of this select group included the Americans Maurice Sendak and Eric Carle, the Netherlands' Dick Bruna, the ronin-like Tomi Ungerer, Japan's Mitsumasa Anno, and a core group of British artists consisting of John Burningham, Brian Wildsmith, the Ahlbergs, Quentin Blake, Raymond Briggs, Shirley Hughes, and Helen Oxenbury, among others.

In Britain the coming-of-age of this new band of picture book artists was part of a larger surge toward cultural renewal. It was as though the war had drained the color from English life and a new generation of artists, designers, musicians, writers, and others had arisen to put it back. As the Beatles would proclaim in much the same celebratory spirit: "Here comes the sun"!

Madcap Scenario

Helen cemented her membership in this group as the illustrator of two books published by Heinemann in 1969: *The Quangle Wangle's Hat*, by Edward Lear, and *The Dragon of an Ordinary Family*, by New Zealand writer Margaret Mahy. The latter tale was a sly upending of the postwar social planners' obsession with normality in all areas of domestic life.

A shaggy-dog story, Mahy's book recounts an average middle-class family's liberating, off-the-chart adventures upon adopting a dragon as a house pet. Helen clearly had fun teasing out the humor in this madcap scenario, introducing the beast, in the cover illustration, as a gentle giant willing to allow family members to use his massive tail as a leaning post, a climbing apparatus, and an umbrella rack.

In the Lear book she easily proved herself a match for the arch Victorian nonsense man's verbal pyrotechnics, fashioning a menagerie of furry and feathery creatures — a mix, as in the text, of the real and the wildly fanciful — that sidle and strut across pages *just* large enough, it seems, to contain them in all their extravagant ridiculousness.

Critics hailed the publication of the two volumes as a major event, and when the time came for the Kate Greenaway Medal committee to confer its laurels, the judges — unable to choose between the books — elected for the first time in the medal's fifteen-year history to award Helen the prize for the two books jointly. If Helen until then had hovered in the shadow of John, she now came into her own with a flourish.

Previous pages and facing page: From The Quangle Wangle's Hat, *Heinemann, 1969*
Next pages: From The Dragon of an Ordinary Family, *Heinemann, 1969*

1970s

Outsider Perspective
A Strong and Forceful Presence
Motherhood and Career
A Great Advance

Outsider Perspective

A frequent visitor to Hampstead in those days was Ivor Cutler, a Glaswegian poet, teacher, and humorist who had attained a cultish sort of fame as a performance artist, especially among college students. Known for his deadpan songs, surreally off-the-wall one-liners, and dyspeptic Scots stage persona, Cutler rarely slipped out of character even as he sipped tea at Helen and John's kitchen table, much less as he cycled the streets of London in an ancient fez or tweed cap adorned with a jaunty sunflower cockade, or with mock solemnity took up his position on a busy street corner to hand out gold stickers stamped with quirky Cutlerisms such as *Befriend a bacterium, True happiness is knowing you're a hypocrite,* and *Please ignore this sign.*

He attracted an impressive array of fans that ranged from Bertrand Russell to Elvis Costello. Even the Beatles came calling to recruit him to play the quizzical bus conductor, Buster Bloodvessel, in their 1967 television film *Magical Mystery Tour.* But Cutler mistrusted success, and as a Scotsman and Jew living in London, he was an odd man out twice over, with an outsider's perspective that served him well when he turned his hand to writing children's books.

Near the end of his life, when an interviewer for a BBC

Previous pages: From Helen's sketchbook, c. 1970

documentary asked, "How do you see yourself?" Cutler, after a long pause, and for once without a shred of irony in his crusty voice, replied, "As a child."

During the 1970s Cutler composed a number of picture book texts; Heinemann published three, all with illustrations by Helen. Although he could often be an exasperating friend, he somehow grasped Helen's need for an absolute ban on casual meddling and mockery. When she, still fearing the worst, finally showed him the finished art for their first collaboration, *Meal One*, she was greatly relieved to find that Cutler had shelved his inner curmudgeon and was prepared to congratulate her on a job well done.

Above: Ivor Cutler, poet, teacher, humorist, and friend of Helen and John

A Strong and Forceful Presence

Meal One gave Helen scope to reflect on the demands of motherhood and family against the backdrop of an outlandish fairy-tale predicament. A boy living with his single mother plants a plum stone in a crack in the floorboards under his bed. No sooner has he done so than a massive tree sprouts root and branch from the stone, rapidly engulfing the house and threatening to disrupt meal one — breakfast to the rest of us — for the boy and his mom.

It is an untenable situation, considering how hungry the two of them are and — more darkly — how nightmarishly overrun their once happy home has suddenly become.

Indeed, all seems lost until this heroic, rough-and-ready mother finds a way to extract them both from their jam by a nimble trick that the reader is not likely to see coming. It delighted Helen to recognize in the story's mom "such a great pal to her son, not your typical worried mother." John would later recognize the boy in the illustrations — Helbert MacHerbert by name — as a slightly caricatured depiction of his and Helen's own son, Bill.

The elaborately blocked-out and furnished interiors, given tonal nuances via sustained bursts of cross-hatching, show the extent to which Helen still approached illustration with her theatrical set designer's hat on tight.

Her drawings of Helbert's stalwart mom as a strong and forceful presence were evidence of her commitment, as well, to progressive views about motherhood and gender stereotypes generally.

The new feminist monthly *Spare Rib* praised *Meal One* for its sympathetic depiction of a capable single mother. No calamity, however dire, would ever likely put this survivor off her stride. As a working mother with a career on the upswing, Helen herself could have wished for no better role model.

Right and next pages:
From Meal One, *Heinemann, 1971*

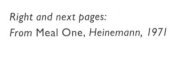

Motherhood and Career

Helen had come of age in the heyday of the British psychiatrist John Bowlby, who urged mothers to embrace their crucial role as the primary shapers of their young children's emotional lives.

For women of Helen's generation with dreams of blending professional fulfillment and family life, Bowlby's message that motherhood and a career were largely incompatible goals came as a blow, with a bad conscience offered up as the likely price for defying the odds. Bowlby's caveat, that a dedicated nanny might fill in part-time for a mother, ignored the question of class, as it was unlikely that the majority of women could afford the right help.

As a working mother herself, Helen had good reason to appreciate the resilience of *Meal One*'s tenacious heroine. Helen had shown resourcefulness of her own by choosing to render the illustrations in crayon rather than watercolor, because crayons were easier to pack up before dinner, when it was time to set aside the day's work and revert to her role as a wife and a mother.

From Meal One, Heinemann, 1971

77

A Great Advance

Helen was lucky enough to begin illustrating picture books just as color printing technology had made great advances. No longer were illustrators obliged to do much of the preparatory work themselves by furnishing the publisher with a series of color studies for each of their illustrations — "separations" that were used as the basis for creating the printer's single-color plates. She was less fortunate in the fact that the position of art director did not yet exist at the British firms, and so when a house undertook to publish a full-color picture book, the task of designing the book usually fell into the lap of the firm's production manager, a staff member whose expertise had more to do with cost-cutting than with striving for aesthetically pleasing outcomes.

Among Helen's next Heinemann projects was one that seemed poised to become a perennial holiday favorite in the great Victorian gift book tradition. *Cakes and Custard*, a treasury of English nursery rhymes, gave the artist an ideal showcase for her

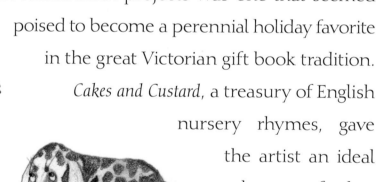

considerable talents for portraiture, animal drawing, and sly situational humor. With scores of pithy lyrics for inspiration, Helen had a field day fashioning a sprawling

rogues' gallery of caricatures: grizzled Desperate Dan, who "washed his face in a frying pan"; the sad, forbearing cow (in "There was a piper") who accepts a piper's tune in lieu of the hay for which she clearly hankers; and a wedding party (for the rhyme "Needles and pins, needles and pins / When a man marries his trouble begins") whose principals resemble suspects in a Miss Marple whodunnit. Adding further luster and a touch of gravitas to the enterprise was the imprimatur of the volume's editor, Brian Alderson, the well-known scholar and critic for *The Times* of London.

Helen submitted the art for *Cakes and Custard* in a great stack of small individual drawings done on card — pieces of a puzzle in need of solving. In the absence of an in-house designer, Jan Pieńkowski agreed to take up the challenge. "Helen," he recalled, "had hit on a brilliant incentive. Every time I managed to get another spread finished and looking OK, she would produce, from her secret hoard, some delicious, exotic choccy items. We would enjoy one or two of these and then discuss some burning question of our time for five minutes maximum, when the whip would come out again and we'd pass on to the next challenge."

Helen's drawing for "The Little Beggar Girl" was a haunting full-length portrait of such raw emotion — a study in tenderness and vulnerability but without a trace of the usual street-waif mawkishness — that Pieńkowski departed from the established pattern of the design and gave the image a page to itself. It was a happy, fruitful collaboration; as Pieńkowski would later write: "Those intense and disciplined days . . . were to become one of the star memories of my design education."

The production of *Cakes and Custard* was another matter entirely. The printer used too much black ink, with the result that all the cross-hatching — and subtlety — of the drawings was lost. The reproduction was so bad that the first printing had to be scrapped and a second run expedited in hopes of catching the all-important end-of-the-year holiday sale. When the new printing proved to be only marginally better, Helen's disappointment was palpable, as it was hard not to read the experience as solid proof that, notwithstanding her own editor's dedication and consummate professionalism, the people in the higher reaches of the house did not care enough about children's books to back their publication in

"The Little Beggar Girl" from Cakes and Custard, Heinemann, 1974

a serious *way*. Loyalty to the house an author had started out with was, however, a golden rule of British publishing culture. Helen, it seemed, had little choice but to soldier on. Or did she?

"I was a Heinemann illustrator until naughty Sebastian came along," Helen would say of this fateful time.

Facing page and above: From Cakes and Custard, *Heinemann, 1974*   **83**

1980s

Charismatic Entrepreneur

"Naughty Sebastian" was Sebastian Walker, a charismatic Mad Hatter and entrepreneur in his mid-thirties whom Helen had first met in Bologna. As Jonathan Cape's European sales representative, Walker had come to Bologna to sell foreign rights to John Burningham's picture books and to entertain Cape authors in attendance at the fair. Ambitious, mercurial, and disinclined to take his place in the family engineering firm, Walker, after a period of drift following his graduation from Oxford, had chanced upon the publishing world, where, regardless of the fact that he did not consider himself to be much of a reader, he saw opportunity wherever he turned. By the time he joined Cape, Walker was the very picture of the young man in a hurry. After learning the business at Cape and at two other houses — Marshall Cavendish and Chatto & Windus, which between them ran the gamut of British publishing from mass market to traditional trade — he struck out on his own. In 1978, with a bank loan secured with his father's help, he established Sebastian Walker Associates and set up shop with a staff of two in the back bedroom of his house in Canonbury, north London.

The war mentality had done much to shape the attitudes of the British publishers of children's books whose ranks Walker now

Previous pages: Working sketches for Big Baby Board Books, c. 1986
Facing page: Sebastian Walker, Walker's founder

joined. During the war and for a long time afterward, they had all been forced to ration materials and learn to make do with less. The pattern, it seemed, had carried over into more prosperous times. During the 1960s a rule remained in place at Heinemann that no children's novel could be longer than forty thousand words. Heinemann's editor, Judith Elliott, had "wanted desperately," as she later recalled, to acquire U.K. rights to Louise Fitzhugh's *Harriet the Spy*, but had been barred from doing so because of this unbending rule.

Thriftiness certainly applied to payment to authors. As a child of the next generation, Walker, however, had not grown up in thrall to the rationing mentality, and as a person given to grand gestures anyway, he believed in a targeted extravagance aimed at achieving a long-term business goal. He first had to prove the firm's viability to the bank. But from then onward, when he came calling, open checkbook in hand, to court a potential artist, writer, or member of staff, few were prepared to resist his largesse.

Friends and detractors alike compared Walker to Mr. Toad from Kenneth Grahame's *The Wind in the Willows* — the incorrigible mischief-maker and irrepressible social being who loved nothing better than to cajole and charm the people around him. The lord of Toad Hall was, however, a hopeless dilettante, whereas Walker, when it came to business, was all business: a super salesman, an uncanny prognosticator of industry trends, and a wizard at dreaming up and implementing unorthodox publishing strategies. People found him fascinating and wanted to get close to the magic, and he quickly assembled a talented young team, starting with an art director he had known

at Cavendish, an American from Brooklyn named Amelia Edwards. "I want to do children's books for the rest of my life," Walker had told Edwards over the phone in a typical breathless rush of unbridled enthusiasm. "Would you like to join me?" Placing an art director at the center of the firm was a key element in Walker's plan to secure the services of the best illustrators from England and beyond.

Other publishers tended to give short shrift to art direction, and it became Edwards's job to make good on Walker's extravagant promises to the artists he brought into the fold by lavishing the utmost care on every aspect of the design and production of their books. With this much of his grand scheme firmly in place, the scene was now perfectly set to bring in Helen Oxenbury.

Above: Amelia Edwards, Walker's founding art director, c. 1980

Making a Splash

Toward the end of 1978 Walker paid his first visit to Helen in Hampstead. When the two casual friends sat down to talk that day, Helen was preoccupied — fully nine months pregnant with her third child — but also looking to the future. They discussed what kinds of books she might *possibly* like to do for Walker.

She recalled with pleasure a clever novelty book she had had growing up, Richard Chopping and Denis Wirth-Miller's *Heads, Bodies and Legs.* It featured three sets of movable paper flaps that allowed the reader to mix and match body parts in a great variety of silly combinations. Helen remembered the little book as an ideal rainy-day distraction — an amusing, unpretentious source of fun — and as a child-friendly cross between a book and a toy. She told Walker that it might interest her to make a book in the same format and spirit.

In the irreverent new age of pop art led by David Hockney and Andy Warhol, and of cutting-edge designers like those at New York's Push Pin Studios and London's Gallery Five, hidebound traditional hierarchies in all areas of the visual arts were rapidly falling away, and a once down-market toy book premise, if carried off with suitable panache, stood a strong chance of making a splash in both

From Animal Allsorts, Methuen/Walker, 1980

aesthetic and commercial terms.

This, it so happened, was precisely the kind of publishing that most intrigued Walker — a dynamic remix of high and low, traditional and pop — and he now proposed that Helen create not one but three such books, noting that each one of the group would, in effect, help to sell the others. When the conversation turned to money, Walker barely had time to propose an advance when Helen waved him off. "Oh, don't bother to give me any money till you've earned a bit," she said, leaving the super salesman uncharacteristically speechless.

Caught short by the better-than-imagined outcome of their

meeting, Walker hastily said his goodbyes, stepped out into the brisk Hampstead air, and proceeded to back his car into a lamp-post. The mishap left a dent that he chose to preserve as a souvenir of what he rightly judged to have been a pivotal moment in the life of his infant firm.

A few weeks later, Helen was in the hospital recovering from childbirth when Walker began turning up at her bedside for daily visits. She later recalled: "I thought, how nice, he's come to see the baby; in fact, he would spend two seconds on the baby and then turn to the artist and ask, 'Now, Helen, when do you think you could get started?'"

Within a few months, Helen had regained her stride and was stealing time for work at the kitchen table. Walker kept his side of the bargain as well by designing and printing the books in a first-rate manner and by pulling in multiple co-editions and ultimately enormous sales.

From Animal Allsorts, Methuen/Walker, 1980

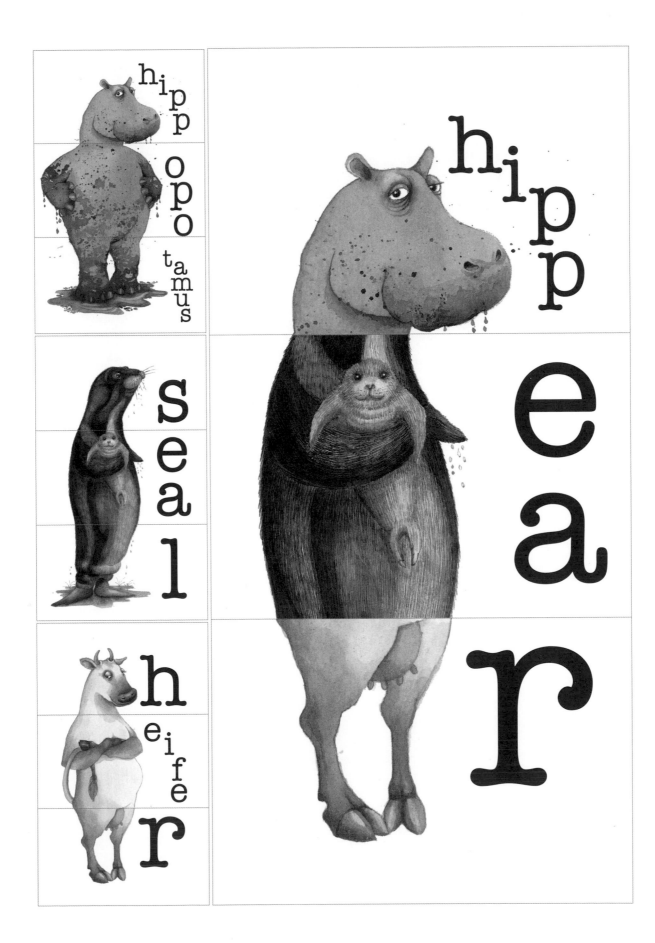

Assurances

Walker then asked Helen what she would like to do next. When she expressed interest in a set of board books for babies, the publisher was thrilled. But before proceeding further, he needed to square things with Heinemann. With this in mind, he paid a courtesy call to Heinemann's Judith Elliott, a ceremonial visit for which he arrived with his powers of persuasion turned up full blast.

"I do hope you don't mind," he began, "but I would so love it if Helen could do just a few little baby books for my list." He spoke of the matter as though he were proposing a short-term loan, and offered his assurances that he expected Helen's long-standing relationship with Heinemann to continue as before.

Elliott took Walker at his word. The Pied Piper, she would later remark, had given the performance of his life, as Walker's true intent had, of course, been to secure the artist's services for the long run. "We were all so nice to each other," Elliott recalled wistfully of that earlier time, when it was common practice for an editor to send "little notes" of congratulation to a rival whenever a book published by the latter won a prize, and when no one even considered "poaching" an author who was firmly established elsewhere. Tom Maschler had perhaps been first to lure artists away from other houses in order to build up the children's books list at Cape. Now, it seemed, Sebastian Walker had set out to out-Maschler Maschler.

Under the circumstances, it was more than a tad ironic that the one project Helen illustrated for Cape was one called *A Child's Book of Manners*, written by Fay Maschler, the publisher's wife. But it would be Sebastian Walker who changed the meaning of "business as usual" forever, and he did so with no compunction whatsoever, convinced as he was that he had come with a fairer deal — and better future — to offer the artists.

First Baby Board Books

Most board books until then were in effect sets of crudely drawn or photographed flash cards with a binding: generic products punched out, without much thought or artistry, to fill a slot in the marketplace. The prevailing assumption was that the genre held little scope for inventiveness in either concept or design. Babies, Helen would recall, had long been "considered vegetable until two years old." Yet her own baby Emily's intense curiosity about the pictures they looked at together in mail-order child care catalogs clearly proved otherwise.

Only two illustrators had taken up the board book as a worthy creative challenge: an American, Rosemary Wells, with her Max and Ruby series; and Dick Bruna of the Netherlands, the creator of Miffy. Helen herself now considered the potential of board books with skillfully organized and well-drawn pictures for an infant to gaze at with growing recognition. She thought hard about what her approach to the genre might be. "Being simple is not that easy, really," she would decide. "I thought a long time about how to do it."

Facing page and next pages: From Dressing, Walker, 1981

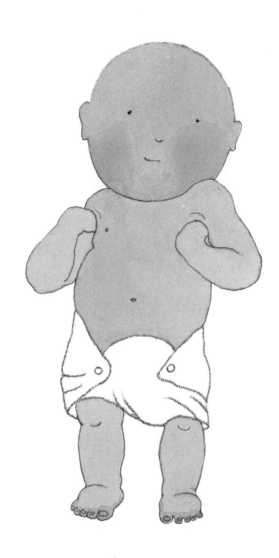

The Wells and Bruna board books both featured fanciful, toy-like bunny characters placed in familiar situations. Helen chose instead to work from the premise that babies take great pleasure in gazing at other babies, whether the encounter occurs across a sandbox, via reflections in a mirror, or through illustrations in a book or magazine.

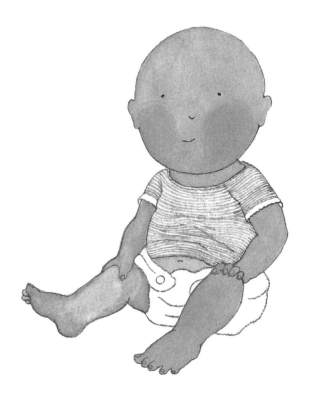

There was much about the first five baby board books published by Walker in 1981 that was wholly original: the degree of care and finesse with which Helen had observed her young subjects and the individuality of their poses and expressions; the naturalness of the situations in which she placed them;

the richness of the humor she had discerned, as though ready-made, in the most everyday circumstances; and the atmosphere of tenderness and love that bound all these elements together in a satisfying way. The books had none of the generic drawing, fuzzy anatomy, random splashes of color, or easy sentiment of the vast majority of books in the genre.

Working in such a distilled, minimalist way meant that even the smallest detail had to be thoroughly considered. "The placement of the dots for eyes was absolutely crucial," Helen recalled. "You had to be so accurate to get it right."

From Helen Oxenbury's Baby Board Books, Methuen/Walker, 1981 & 1983; Sainsbury's/Walker, 1985

Working
Helen Oxenbury

Playing
Helen Oxenbury

Family
Helen Oxenbury

Shopping
Helen Oxenbury

Helping
Helen Oxenbury

Bedtime
Helen Oxenbury

I touch
Helen Oxenbury

I see
Helen Oxenbury

Cultural Shifts and Trends

Psychologists had redoubled their efforts during the postwar years to understand every aspect of young children's growth and development. Among the surprises to emerge was the finding that reading to children from the time of birth yielded long-term benefits for the healthy development of brain function.

News of this discovery made the rounds just as the grown-up children of the postwar baby boom years were starting families of their own. The new 1980s parents were better educated and more book-minded than those of previous generations, and they readily accepted the experts' advice. Thus, when Helen proposed her first baby book series to Sebastian Walker, he saw clearly that she was onto something: the books would fill a rising demand in the market. As it turned out, worldwide interest in the first set of Helen Oxenbury board books was so strong that the initial sales were enough to put Walker's new company on a firm financial footing well ahead of schedule.

In 1979, having outgrown the upstairs back bedroom in the founder's own house, Walker Books moved to its first proper offices, in a half-hidden London side street between the major commercial thoroughfares of Tottenham Court Road and Oxford

Street. Walker had chosen an idiosyncratic, frill-free, loft-like space, a former sweatshop that sat directly above an Indian restaurant.

Access was by way of an iron fire escape where pots of curry were routinely left to cool and discarded fish heads made the spot a favorite with the neighborhood cats — and rats. It was a world away from the hushed precincts of nearby literary Bloomsbury, and, partly for that reason, book people, Helen among them, looked forward to their visits as they might to any adventure. Sebastian, it was said, would sweep all those old bones away when an important artist or American publisher came.

Inside the premises, there were lines of windows. The then unconventional open-plan office, vases of fresh flowers placed on every desk, and in-house chef and communal lunch table fostered a spirit of camaraderie.

Helen observed: "With some publishers you become a bit of a nuisance when you come into the office, but Walker Books was completely the opposite. Didn't someone in a publisher's once say, 'We ought to have a special room set aside for authors and illustrators because they do get under your feet when they come in'? You never felt that with Walker Books." Another major draw was the art director. As Helen recalled, "You couldn't *not* like Amelia."

Sebastian Walker's favorite reading material was said to be his company's sales reports, which, much like the books he published, typically had a happy ending. He rarely involved himself in editorial matters except insofar as he edited his staff and — as in the case of Helen — took the lead in wooing an artist or writer he was convinced Walker Books needed to publish. In the first years, he hired a number of Americans, in part with a view to making sure that the books would go down well in America, where by the early 1980s a second baby boom was under way, independent children's bookshops and preschools were proliferating in response to the burgeoning demand, and the nation's public libraries were for the first time opening their doors to the board book audience and their caretakers.

An early Walker Books catalog featuring Helen's new First Experiences series on the cover

A Spirit of Fun

Another early Walker hire was editor
David Lloyd, an author of merry picture
book texts who had read Japanese
literature at Oxford, been a drummer
in a band, and worked in nonfiction
publishing before going out on the road
as a clown in an old-fashioned traveling
circus. The last experience may well have
been the best preparation of all for editing

picture books, an art form similarly performance-based, intimate
in scale, and meant to hold children's attention in a spirit of fun.

A picture book text is a performance in the making, and it
was among Lloyd's special talents to be able to *hear* the potential
in a manuscript and, by reading it aloud, to convey that potential
to others.

It soon became an important part of his job, whenever a
manuscript that might be right for Helen to illustrate came into
the office, for Lloyd to set out for Hampstead to read the text to
her over lunch at a restaurant. When the editor reached the end
of one of these performances, he would then attempt to gauge

Above: David Lloyd, Helen's editor at Walker   **105**

Helen's interest, hoping, of course, for a simple yes. The artist, however, being quick to grasp the difficulties posed by a given text, typically preferred not to commit herself on the spot. Before long, a joke arose between them that unless Helen agreed to Lloyd's suggestion, there would be "no pudding" that day.

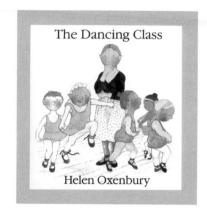

Lloyd was not only the ideal reader; for the stories originated by Helen, he was the ideal coauthor as well. On visits to Hampstead, he and Helen would work closely to revise or polish whatever manuscript of Helen's was at hand. The first of these sessions took place one afternoon in late 1981. Sebastian Walker had asked Lloyd to "help with the words" for a new picture book called *The Dancing Class*, the first of a series of small books about episodes in a young child's life. Others in the series would include *The Birthday Party*, *Eating Out*, *The Drive*, *The Check-up*, and *Playschool*, all published in 1983. Lloyd had been with the house for less than a year, but he had known Helen's books long before that as a parent who read to his children.

The chance now to work with their creator seemed an exciting prospect indeed. "Helen," Lloyd recalled, "had already plotted out the book and made some first sketches; she may

Helen Oxenbury's First Experiences Picture Books, Walker, 1983 & 1984

The Drive

Helen Oxenbury

The Visitor

Helen Oxenbury

The Check-up

Helen Oxenbury

Gran and Grandpa

Helen Oxenbury

Our Dog

Helen Oxenbury

Eating Out

Helen Oxenbury

even have finished some colored art. Only the *words* were missing."

Wonderful Humor

As Emily Burningham — the immediate inspiration for her mother's first two sets of board books — advanced up the ladder from baby and toddlerhood to the preschool years, Helen kept pace at her drawing table, creating books suggested by her daughter's experiences. The new series was to focus on children ready to venture out into the world, and whose greater physical and mental capacity rendered them at once more adept at mischief-making and more vulnerable to being misjudged by their parents. The comic potential in all this, Helen realized, was endless.

The drawings Lloyd saw that day made a strong impression. "What was immediately obvious," he recalled, "was the truth and accuracy of Helen's observations, and the wonderful humor.

"A child attending her first ballet class takes a tumble while dancing, in an excess of enthusiasm; then all the other pupils fall over. Look at the concerned faces, look at the crumpled pink tights, look at the grubby feet!"

A seemingly minor detail in one of the drawings suddenly crystallized for Lloyd the full extent of Helen's uncanny powers of observation. The pianist, a heavyset older woman, wore a support bandage around her calf. In so "simple" a picture book about a little girl's first foray into the realm of dance, here was a touch of realism that went well beyond the literal requirements of the situation — a subtle aside (if one thought about it) on the vagaries of physical decline. Just then Lloyd was reminded that the pianist at the dance class *he* had attended as a child had worn a similar bandage, and that the curious spectacle of it had piqued his interest. "Does Helen have a direct line into my life?" he thought as he grasped the larger point.

That bandage aside, the remarkable thing about the illustrations laid out before him was their resolutely child's-eye perspective.

Facing page and next pages: From The Dancing Class, *Walker, 1983*

Helen's gift was her ability to home in on the pictorial elements of greatest interest to a child and discern the universal dimension in the ordinary.

Mishaps

Helen would later say, "I think that children like mishaps, especially when they occur to the grown-ups." In the books for preschool children, she had great fun exploring the comic consequences of this proposition, dramatizing instances of the broad gap that often lies between adult ideas about what is fun for a child and children's own ideas about this. Out for a family meal amid a commotion of restaurant servers and breakable items, a child prefers to crawl under the table and manages in slapstick fashion to trip the waiter. During an interminable family car ride, a child finally reaches the breaking point of endurance and boredom, turns queasy, and throws up. The helter-skelter unraveling is the comic payoff and, for parents, a gentle reminder as well to give due consideration to the child's point of view. "It is impossible," Helen would tell an interviewer, "to be too much on the side of the child."

Every afternoon, Emily returned home from school and headed

From **The Drive**, Walker, 1983

Above: From Playschool, Walker, 1983
Facing page: From The Check-up, Walker, 1983

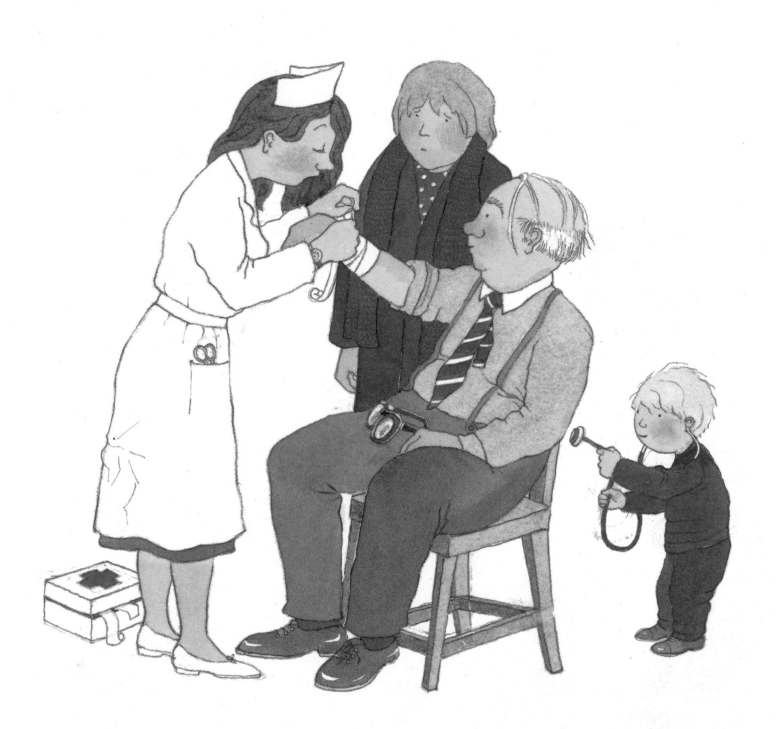

straight to her mother's upstairs studio, where she would watch in wonder as Helen calmly and confidently applied daubs of watercolor to a drawing. As a young schoolgirl, Emily now had artwork of her own to do, and it later amused her to recall the times when Helen, reverting despite herself into professional artist mode, would act on the urge to "improve" her daughter's drawing, if only ever so slightly.

"Why, Emily," — wink, wink! — "you have done such a fine job!" the teacher might comment in class the next day.

The World's Children

Helen went from strength to strength as she continued to experiment with the board book genre. As her worldwide audience expanded, she also began to know more of her publishers from abroad. Among these was Dial Press's Phyllis Fogelman, the New York–based editor who had first introduced Helen's board books to the American market and who made regular trips to London.

An ardent champion of progressive political causes and a pugnacious businesswoman, Fogelman was best known in the States for having successfully made the case for publishing children's books that celebrated America's racial diversity. It was perhaps a

Helen painting with her daughter Emily, c. 1983

serendipitous mark of this cultural shift toward greater inclusion that Helen remarked one day to Amelia Edwards on the need for books for "babies of every color" — books that acknowledged and celebrated the racial diversity of the world's children. A new set of four big board books grew out of the conversation. *Clap Hands, Say Goodnight, Tickle, Tickle,* and *All Fall Down* had rounded corners and a larger-than-typical format that allowed for frieze-like drawings featuring animated groupings of three or four toddlers and the occasional parent or caregiver. Helen outlined the figures not in standard black ink but rather in pencil, an unusual choice that heightened the drawings' intimacy.

The figures were cropped in an unconventional, off-center way as well, with one or more of the children often shown standing up or toddling out of the picture frame, as a small child might be seen to do in a family snapshot. The effect

Above: From Clap Hands, *Walker, 1987*
Facing page: From All Fall Down, *Walker, 1987*

of all this was to maximize the dynamic energy of drawings in which Helen paid close attention to the fledgling interactions of four little youngsters who, though still very much the center of their own worlds, were nonetheless also becoming keenly aware of one another. No previous book meant for children of the youngest ages had ever taken so close a look at the social dimension of small children's lives. But here were four happy toddlers of diverse racial backgrounds swinging in their swings, prancing around in circles, and curling up together at naptime, all perfectly at home with one another.

Next pages: From Clap Hands, All Fall Down, Tickle, Tickle, *and* Say Goodnight, Walker, *1987*

Clap Hands

Helen Oxenbury

Clap hands, dance and spin,

open wide and pop it in,

blow a trumpet, bang a drum,

wave to Daddy, wave to Mum.

All Fall Down

Helen Oxenbury

Singing all together,

running round and round,

bouncy, bouncy, on the bed,

all fall down.

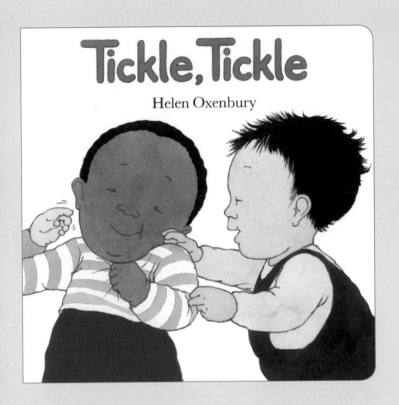

Squelch, squelch, in the mud,

splish, splash, scrub-a-dub,

gently, gently, brush your hair,

tickle, tickle, under there.

Up, down, up in the sky,

swing low, swing high,

bumpetty, bumpetty, hold on tight,

hush, little babies, say goodnight.

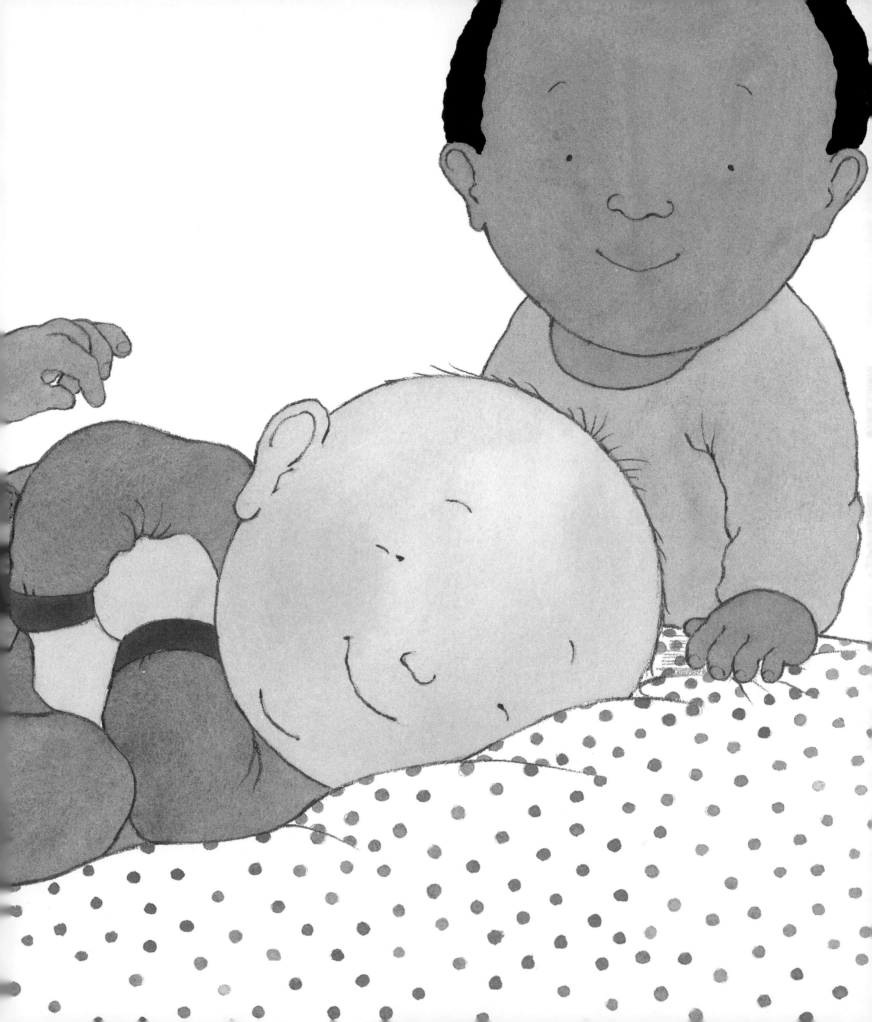

1990s

The First Time

In 1977 the well-known Scottish folk singer Alison McMorland came to Hampstead to ask Helen if she would design the record sleeve for an album of traditional children's songs. McMorland, who had brought along her guitar, performed some of the songs from *The Funny Family* and was rewarded for her efforts with an enthusiastic yes. Just one drawing, Helen thought, and the job would be done! It seemed a refreshing change from the marathon effort of picture book illustration. Among the old songs she heard for the first time that day was one called "We're Going on a Bear Hunt."

Serendipitously, it was at about this same time that the poet and performer Michael Rosen came across the song too, and liked it well enough to incorporate it into the one-man show he performed for schoolchildren all around Britain. Years passed. Then one day, while listening from his place in the audience at one of Rosen's performances, David Lloyd, who was also Rosen's Walker editor, recognized the song's potential as a picture book text for Helen to illustrate.

Rosen at first did not see how it could be done and resisted Lloyd's suggestion. As Rosen later recalled: "I said that he should

Previous pages: Early sketches for The Three Little Wolves and the Big Bad Pig, *c. 1992*
Facing page: Helen and her family, c. 1978. From right to left: Stanley the dog, husband John, daughter Lucy, son Bill, Helen, and, in her arms, daughter Emily

write it down. He said I should. I said that he should. He said that I should. So I did." Realizing that the traditional text needed some fleshing out, Rosen added the "Splash splosh!" and other sound effects that came to punctuate the now well-known version, as well as two additional scenes: the "Stumble trip!" through the forest and the snowstorm "Hoooo woooo!"

Scenes and Settings

Helen's practice until then had been the standard one of completing the first few drawings for a book and then bringing them into her publisher's office for discussion.

This time, however, she chose to do things differently, keeping more or less entirely to herself during

From We're Going on a Bear Hunt, *Walker, 1989*

the eighteen or so months it took to complete the illustrations and map out the design. She chose the trim size, an unusually large one for the time. She decided to alternate watercolor illustrations (for the action adventure scenes) with pencil drawings (for the times when the family is considering the problem) and to place a black-and-white drawing against an all-white background on the jacket, another highly unconventional choice that made for a classically clear and understated impression.

The final effect was of a book that had seemingly not been printed but rather hand-drawn as a gift for a particular child. Rosen would later say that he had imagined a fairy-tale setting for the

Above and next pages: From We're Going on a Bear Hunt, *Walker, 1989*

text with perhaps a bumbling king leading the bear hunt, followed by a helter-skelter entourage of courtier huntsmen. He did not have the chance to express this view in advance, however, nor did Helen seek his advice. In fact, in her total absorption with her drawings, she forgot to leave any room at all for the text. "That is why in the end the main picture — the watercolor — is almost always on the right," she recalled with a laugh, "and is continued on the left behind a sort of block within which the text is framed." It was Helen's son, Bill, then employed as a designer at Walker Books, who came up with the solution.

One reason Helen felt so engaged by the text was that it gave her the chance to bring landscape into her work following a long run of books for babies and toddlers for which featureless (or nearly so) monochromatic backgrounds had been key elements of the age-appropriate design. For the illustrations of *We're Going on a Bear Hunt*, she could now open her art wide to the myriad forms and textures of place.

Not surprisingly, certain landscapes interested her more than others. Scenes and settings were remembered from near and far. The forest was the wooded area just beyond her doorstep in Hampstead Heath. The rocky shoreline — home to the bear — was the rugged coast of Druidstone, Pembrokeshire, in southwest Wales, where she and her family had once walked on holiday.

But it was the mudflats through which the wayfarers of *Bear Hunt* slip and slide under a steel-gray sky that meant the most to her personally. This, after all, was a scene straight out of her own Felixstowe days, her teenage stomping ground with its stark beauty, sharp, crisp air, "very particular quality of light, clearer and brighter than in the south and west of England," and its "huge variety of wading birds." This to her was the place that epitomized the freedom to be young, on one's own, and on the lookout for adventure.

The realism of the illustrations, while palpable, was of course also selective. Asked once why she had put old tires and a discarded tin can into some of them, Helen replied: "Because this is what you find. I can remember having more fun as a child throwing stones at a tin can on the beach [as the six- or seven-year-old boy in *We're Going on a Bear Hunt* does] than from playing with any expensive toy." Some parents, she noted, "feel that they're not good parents if they don't buy expensive toys." At the core of Helen's vision of childhood was the belief that imagination is an inner resource to be nurtured, not a thing to be bought.

Comings and Goings

To Helen's pleasure, Rosen's text left much to her discretion. "We're never told who 'we' are," she later observed, "so it is entirely up to the illustrator to create the characters. The scenes with the snowstorm and the mud are also never described, so again it was up to me to decide how they looked.

"Then the bear: we're not told what sort of bear it is, whether fierce or friendly." She resolved the last dilemma when a publishing friend of hers who was going through personal difficulties came to live temporarily in Hampstead in the house next door to Helen's.

Ever observant, the artist noted her forlorn friend's dejection and applied it to the bear in the tale.

Finding a graphic equivalent for the rhythm and pacing of Rosen's words presented another challenge. "The text has a wonderful way of gathering speed, so I had to find a way of not letting the illustrations slow down. That's why it becomes like a strip cartoon toward the end as the family rush back home with the bear at their heels."

Helen continued to wonder about the bear. It became important to her to know his backstory. She recalled in the *Guardian*: "It occurred to me three-quarters of the way through that possibly the bear was all on his own in the cave, and might just have wanted some company rather than to eat the children." In the dramatic moonlit scene printed on the closing endpapers, the bear, with his back to the viewer, slopes off into the night, looking utterly downcast. This comes as a kind of coda for readers to discover on their own. The sudden pivot from suspense to pathos lends the story an unexpectedly poignant added dimension. In that one unscripted moment, a merry song of innocence becomes a song of experience as well.

A Signal Event

The British and American editions of *We're Going on a Bear Hunt* were released simultaneously in the autumn of 1989, the latter by Margaret K. McElderry Books, the eponymous Macmillan imprint of the gallant, fun-loving doyenne of the American children's book publishing industry. An Anglophile in good standing who had served in Europe as a military intelligence officer during the Second World War, McElderry was among the first of the ardent internationalists and Bologna enthusiasts. Well into her seventies, she continued to personally oversee a highly selective list and hold court regularly for influential librarians and reviewers, who had long since learned to anticipate any book that appeared under her banner as a signal event. *Bear Hunt*'s introduction as the lead title on the all-important McElderry holiday season list could not help but amplify the attention the book was bound to receive anyway. When Helen toured the United States that November, journalists, librarians, and parents with children in tow lined up in droves to meet her.

Although few people were in a position to notice it, the U.K. and U.S. editions of *Bear Hunt* arrived on shop shelves with different cover designs. The understated Walker jacket, meticulously prepared

Quick! Back through the cave! Tiptoe! Tiptoe! Tiptoe!

Back through the snowstorm! Hoooo wooooo! Hoooo wooooo!

Back through the forest! Stumble trip! Stumble trip! Stumble trip!

Back through the mud! Squelch squerch! Squelch squerch!

Back through the river! Splash splosh! Splash splosh! Splash splosh!

Back through the grass! Swishy swashy! Swishy swashy!

by Helen herself, featured an intimate black-and-white drawing of the five young "hunters" and their dog marching across the front and back of the wraparound jacket. For the American edition — whether it was McElderry's decision or that of the newly assertive marketing executives she, like her counterparts at the other large houses, increasingly had to contend with — the jacket illustration had been finished in color.

Helen felt *We're Going on a Bear Hunt* marked a great leap forward for her. In an interview, she compared the advance to breakthroughs she had experienced decades earlier as a Junior Wimbledon tennis player: a sudden conquest of once insurmountable barriers and a heady sense of having acquired new strength, focus, stamina, and mastery. She was feeling energized and keen to continue along this fresh path when David Lloyd called to invite her to lunch. A new story had come in that he thought she might like to hear.

Facing page, top: Front cover design for U.K. first edition of We're Going on a Bear Hunt
Facing page, bottom: Front cover design for U.S. first edition of We're Going on a Bear Hunt
Next pages: From We're Going on a Bear Hunt, *Walker, 1989*

FARMER DUCK

Martin Waddell • Helen Oxenbury

Animals Rebelling

The story, called *Farmer Duck*, was by Martin Waddell, and it struck Helen immediately that it possessed the two essential ingredients she watched for in a picture book text: it was funny and it was true. Waddell had written a playful story about a perennial childhood concern — unfairness. Adding further to its interest, the author's fable about farmyard animals banding together to rebel against a lazy, loutish farmer also read as political satire. Adults and children were each given a way in. Still, Helen hesitated. Scrambling to imagine the work that lay ahead for her if she said yes, she questioned whether she was capable of recasting a duck as a nimble farm laborer and forceful leader. She decided to mull the question over. Two weeks passed before Helen told Lloyd she would give the book a try.

The tradition of grafting human attributes onto imaginary creatures from the animal world is older than Aesop. The illusion always entails a sleight of hand, and more ways than one have been found to make the trick work. In a letter explaining why he

Facing page and right: From Farmer Duck, Walker, *1991*

had declined to allow Walt Disney to animate *Charlotte's Web*, E. B. White laid out the polar extremes of the available options: "My feeling about animals," White remarked, "is just the opposite of Disney's. He made them dance to his tune. . . . I preferred to dance to their tune."

Helen stood firmly with White — and Beatrix Potter — on this matter. Her method, like theirs, was to start from close observation of animals in nature, then to remain on the alert for chances to endow the characters modeled on them with human-like powers of feeling, thought, and expression.

A slight curling of a duck's wing feathers, Helen found, was quite enough to make a persuasive visual case for the bird's ability to grasp a hoe. (Disney had simply clapped a pair of rubbery hands onto Donald Duck.)

Helen drew her duck with meticulously placed single-dot eyes and, through the addition of a few minimal worry lines, gave her

From Farmer Duck, *Walker, 1991*

159

feathery farm laborer the furrowed brow of somebody with much on her mind.

As Helen worked on *Farmer Duck* and considered "what expression of tiredness the duck should have on its face," she produced a stack of drawings far thicker than the book itself. In the end, the magic of the *Farmer Duck* illustrations lay in the seeming naturalness with which all the various farmyard characters inhabited their unnatural roles.

This too was the theater of illustration — playful, pointed, and a touch surreal — its dramatic impact immeasurably enhanced by the rhapsodic realism of background landscapes bathed in a particular weather and light. In a world so convincingly rendered, the sheer misery of the dogged duck leading a cow through the rain became something the reader could almost feel.

Above, left, facing page, and next pages: From Farmer Duck, *Walker, 1991*

There was much to smile at as well: the cow's
ingenious method of "sitting down" on a hay bale
without crushing her udder; the deluxe ice
cream sundae prepared by the duck for
the ungrateful farmer, festive cocktail
umbrella and all, as much as to
say that this duck, like the
artist responsible for her, was
not about to miss a trick.

Fondest Dreams

Farmer Duck was Walker's lead title for the autumn 1991 season, and in the spring of the following year it also topped the inaugural list of the firm's shiny new American outpost, Candlewick Press. (The Walker name had long since been taken in the United States by another publishing firm.) Sebastian Walker had always made publishing across national markets the linchpin of his business strategy, and he regarded the U.S. market as the biggest prize of all. Expansion of the company into America was among his fondest dreams and top long-term priorities. "I can't wait," he declared with his usual Walker flair, "for the American tail to wag the English dog!"

Walker laid ambitious plans for the first Candlewick list, persuading the preeminent American illustrator, Maurice Sendak, to collaborate with Iona Opie on *I Saw Esau* and buying back the American rights to the phenomenally successful *Where's Waldo?* books from Little, Brown. As the time approached to open up shop in the United States, he turned over planning responsibilities to managing director David Ford, the American who would head the U.S. operation. Ford chose to bypass New York in favor of offices in the historic college town of Cambridge, Massachusetts. The surprise move only served to burnish the company's reputation for idiosyncratic flair and lightning-quick trend-spotting. What was Walker Books on to — or up to — now?

Tragically, Sebastian Walker's dazzling run was about to come to an untimely end. In autumn 1989, Walker had been diagnosed as HIV-positive; he died two years later, just months before the first Candlewick list went out to the world. On learning he was terminally ill, Walker made a characteristically ingenious and far-reaching decision: to ensure that the firm whose independence he had vigorously safeguarded would never fall into the hands of some corporate colossus, he formally transferred ownership of the house to its authors, illustrators, and staff. He could take satisfaction in the knowledge that there was much to preserve. In twelve years, the company had grown into a seventeen-million-pound business that published three hundred new books annually.

In June 1992, Helen flew to Boston for the first leg of a whirlwind eleven-state "American Heartland" tour to promote *Farmer Duck* and herald the arrival of a lively new British-born publishing imprint on American soil. In keeping with the book's rural theme (and the firm's reputation for idiosyncratic thinking), Helen's itinerary charted a course primarily through farming communities in Vermont, Kentucky, Tennessee, and Kansas, along with stops in

Los Angeles and San Francisco. Bookshops had been challenged to devise the most *Farmer Duck*–appropriate welcome, and Helen soon found herself the honored guest at old-timey small-town parades and petting zoos, barbecues and square dances. She came away from one such event with the key to the city of Noblesville, Indiana.

One-off Portraits

After the intense and protracted effort that was required to create the parallel farmyard universe of Martin Waddell's satirical fantasy, Helen felt ready for a change. Somewhat to her own surprise, she took out her oil paints, a medium she had enjoyed exploring in college but had not worked in for a great many years, and began painting a series of one-off portraits. Among these was a probing likeness of her daughter Lucy, now a young artist herself. Oil, unlike watercolor, is a forgiving medium; painting in oils allowed Helen the luxury of revising at will without having to start over from the beginning.

As she worked and reworked these for-her-eyes-only portraits, she let her mind float a bit and wondered what might be next for her as an illustrator.

Helen's oil portrait of her daughter Lucy, c. 1992

Clever Animals

Helen was in a mood to continue her renewed exploration of oils when her original publisher, Heinemann, sent over a picture book manuscript that greatly intrigued her. A classic nursery tale turned on its head, *The Three Little Wolves and the Big Bad Pig* presented a fresh chance to draw high-spirited animal characters in human situations, as Helen had recently done with such finesse in *Farmer Duck*. The latter book had aptly been called a sort of junior version of George Orwell's *Animal Farm*.

The new manuscript likewise hinted at darker undercurrents beneath its sparkling surface: a sense of a fractured, off-kilter world where ordinary folk (represented by, of all things, a trio of amiable wolves) live in constant fear behind ever-stronger walls.

The author of this provocative tale was not only one of Greece's best-known writers for children but also a sociologist renowned for his studies of crowd psychology and criminal behavior. Helen found that she agreed wholeheartedly with Eugene Trivizas's forthright recipe for a less fearful society: fewer barriers of all kinds between people and more and better communication. The story had other appeals for her as well. "Wolves get bad press," she recalls

From **The Three Little Wolves and the Big Bad Pig**, *Heinemann, 1993*

having thought at the time, "but in fact they are wonderful and clever animals." Here was a chance to depict this much-maligned creature in a sympathetic light.

Helen sketched and re-sketched the illustrations as she worked toward discovering the most dramatic option for each scene. In one of the first shuttlecock scene sketches, she placed the bellicose pig squarely in the foreground. "Then I thought it would be more spooky — and telling — to have the pig just appearing above the wall, hardly visible at all, with only one of the wolves catching sight of him." When she could not get the wolves to come right in the drawing where they huddle in fear and trembling by their window, she photographed John and Lucy in the pose. "It was absolutely hilarious," Helen recalls. "There they were — clutching each other and trying hard to look terrified."

For the sequence in which the wolves replace their cozy brick cottage with a fortresslike modern concrete structure, Helen's research took her to London's South Bank.

The sprawling Royal National Theatre complex, built in the 1970s in the brutalist style then in fashion, seemed to epitomize the bleakness and impersonality of contemporary life that the story satirized. "Actually, I'm quite fond of that building now," Helen says.

From **The Three Little Wolves and the Big Bad Pig**, *Heinemann, 1993*

"But at the time, I thought it was quite awful: concrete blocks — bunkers."

Helen completed the illustrations, but not without harboring a lingering doubt that rendering the art in dark, heavy oils might have been a big mistake. Before long, her visiting American publisher Margaret K. McElderry confirmed her worst fears. "It's fine, Helen, if that is how you really want to do the illustrations, but I'm afraid I won't be publishing it." Helen started the illustrations again, this time in watercolor, which felt so much better.

Even so, going back to square one had to have been difficult. "John said, 'I don't know how you can do that.' But I thought, when it's not right, it's not right." In the end, *The Three Little Wolves and the Big Bad Pig* would stand out for Helen as one of her favorite projects.

Facing page and right: From The Three Little Wolves and the Big Bad Pig, *Heinemann, 1993*

Domestic Bliss

Before long there was another lunch with David Lloyd. A manuscript had come to Walker from a London-based writer well known as a cast member of the popular Children's BBC program *Playdays*. A self-described "daydreamer," Trish Cooke had grown up in West Yorkshire, a child of Afro-Caribbean parents, and had trained for a career in theater. While in college, she had also tried her hand at various kinds of writing — the children's picture book among them.

The manuscript of *So Much* showed a sure grasp of the genre. Cooke constructed the story as an accumulative tale in which members of a large extended Afro-Caribbean family gather one by one to celebrate a father's birthday. It was a universal story, but Cooke's subtle suggestion of dialect — an unusual choice for a picture book of the time — also made it an affirmation of cultural pride. As a performance piece, it worked like a charm. By the time Lloyd had completed his bravura reading over lunch — a recital for which intrigued diners and waiters alike had apparently stopped what they were doing — Helen was smiling broadly and her editor knew that he had his answer.

Left and facing page: From So Much, *Walker, 1994*

Helen was pleased as always to have a manuscript in which the setting was left largely to her discretion. For this story in which people and their relationships had pride of place, she

opted for comparatively plain backdrops: the simply furnished room interiors of a modest single-family house. Her most striking decision was to choose gouache rather than the medium of transparent watercolor with which she was so closely identified. Gouache was less delicate in impact than watercolor but also a good deal more emphatic, and for this reason seemed better suited to a story that grew more animated with the onstage arrival of each new character. Before long, a bold plum-red interior wall had become a vibrant backdrop for the action in several scenes.

A strong, clear design, suggested by the highly structured text,

Above and facing page: From So Much, *Walker, 1994*

soon emerged. Exuberant, big full-color paintings would fill nearly every right-hand page. In counterpoint to these, small black-and-white spot illustrations, most of the baby of the family, would be placed on nearly every left-hand page, just below or alongside the text. As a second pacing device, Helen introduced a series of muted three-color illustrations that marked the calmer in-between moments in the story when family members paused to await the next arrival.

From a design standpoint, *So Much* was a kind of elegant three-part invention. More than this, however, it was Helen's new palette that attracted comment, at first sight surprising everyone, from the staff at Walker to the critics who had come to know and admire her as the quintessential English line and water-color artist. It was as though — nearly three full decades into her career — Helen Oxenbury had reinvented herself as a colorist.

Helen's strength as a portrait artist helped her meet the greatest challenge posed by Cooke's manuscript: the need to be right about everything to do with the story's characters — their

Left and facing page: From So Much, *Walker, 1994*

expressions, body language, hairstyles, dress — all the details that a cultural outsider, even one as observant and empathetic as Helen, might easily get wrong. Recognizing that she had a lot to learn, Helen talked at length with Cooke and went to Brixton, the largely Afro-Caribbean section of south London, wandering the streets, stopping in cafés, observing the people around her, and remembering what she saw.

Brixton had made headlines in recent times of recession and high unemployment as the scene of deadly clashes between disaffected members of the immigrant community and the Metropolitan Police. *So Much* — a notably upbeat picture book — had nothing directly to say about the ongoing racial tensions there and around the United Kingdom. Even so, Cooke's celebratory tale of family cohesion and domestic harmony could be read as an implicit response to those in Thatcher Britain who wished to believe that the people of Brixton and places like it were somehow less caring, or humanly worthy, than people elsewhere.

Helen's portrait-painting interlude had, as it turned out, prepared her well for this latest development. She painted the illustrations confidently and with renewed conviction.

Facing page and right: From So Much, *Walker, 1994*

When award season rolled around, *So Much* took the Smarties Book Prize in the five and under category and the Kurt Maschler Award, named after the father of the editor at Jonathan Cape who had launched John Burningham's career so many years earlier.

Alice's
Adventures in Wonderland
LEWIS CARROLL

HELEN OXENBURY

Wonderland and Beyond

A Nashville reporter had asked Helen during her 1992 American tour if there was some classic children's book she longed to illustrate. *"Alice,"* she replied without hesitation, adding that she would never "dare" to do it. Helen had been giving the question of an *Alice* edition considerable thought for years.

The possibility had first been broached in the early 1980s, when an editor Helen knew from Heinemann ascended to the top spot at Puffin. On a visit to the Burninghams in Hampstead, Liz Attenborough had begun the business portion of the get-together by securing John's agreement to illustrate a new Puffin edition of *The Wind in the Willows.* Attenborough then turned to Helen. Was there an old standard that she might wish to take on? Helen's first response was an unpromising "No, thank you." In the case of a classic, Helen explained, she found it impossible to think of the text apart from the illustrations originally associated with it.

Attenborough replied that she could well understand Helen's feeling about this. "Still," she pressed on, rolling the dice one more time, "if you had to choose, which would it be?"

Facing page and right: From Alice's Adventures in Wonderland, *Walker, 1999*

"Well, possibly *Alice*. . . ." said Helen. "That would be perfect!"

Attenborough left Hampstead savoring her double triumph. As it turned out, however, work on Helen's *Alice* did not start anytime soon. A major stumbling block was her inability to visualize the Alice she might wish to draw. Having an image of her protagonist firmly in mind as both model and muse was for Helen an absolute precondition, a necessary hurdle to be cleared, and Helen was prepared to wait for as long as it took for her Alice to present herself. Years went by, punctuated by occasional social gatherings where the editor might venture gingerly, "Have you found your Alice, Helen?" The rueful answer would always be the same. Still, the idea of a new *Alice* refused to go away.

Then one day everything seemed to snap into place.

Attenborough's firm had become an arm of media giant Pearson, whose other properties included a television production company and broadcast operation. Keen to collaborate, the Pearson book and television people held a brainstorming session at which admiring words were spoken about Lewis Carroll—and Helen Oxenbury. Before long, Helen had been engaged to create sketches for an *Alice* mega-project destined for both page and screen.

The timing struck Helen as uncanny. At a recent garden party

Previous pages and facing page: From Alice's Adventures in Wonderland, *Walker, 1999*

wedding she had attended, she had seen a young girl she felt really was her Alice. The mountain had moved! Helen had made sure to take a photo of the girl.

Media giants are notoriously unreliable creatures, however. Some months after Helen submitted her sketches came the awful news that Pearson's broadcast division had lost its license, which meant that the television *Alice* could not go forward, and that Attenborough had moved on from Pearson, which doomed the book possibility as well. It was then that Helen invited David Lloyd and Amelia Edwards to her studio, showed them the character studies for the television *Alice*, and proposed that, since the program had been canceled, perhaps Walker would like to make the book. They agreed on the spot. It had been a long way around to an outcome that in retrospect seemed inevitable.

That matter settled, the real work began: the quest for a way to escape the powerful gravitational pull of Sir John Tenniel's iconic drawings. The Tenniel illustrations had long since burned themselves into pop-cultural consciousness through endless recyclings on posters, coffee mugs, T-shirts, and the like, as well as, of course, the printed page.

As Helen began sketching, however, she had more than a snapshot image of her Alice to guide her. She had been giving careful thought to the question of how *Alice*'s readership, and the experience of childhood, had changed over the past near century and a half. For one thing, Carroll's classically educated first readers had grown up in a more bookish age than our own. (Alice, at seven, is described as having already studied both Latin and French.)

It was therefore no surprise that the artist chosen by Carroll himself had given his Alice such a coolly appraising look. The Tenniel illustrations had satirical wit to spare but were arguably too remote — perhaps even too un-child-friendly — for turn-of-the-new-millennium children.

With this in mind and starting from the advantage of full-color art, Helen clothed her Alice in plain white tennis shoes and a blue tank-top dress and gave her the thoughtful but wide-eyed, open expression of a girl that any young reader might know. It was just that this girl happened to have the extraordinary luck to tumble down a rabbit hole to a place beyond her wildest imaginings.

A second point had to do with a sea change in attitudes toward the value the adult world placed on childhood curiosity and imagination. In Victorian times, classroom learning had typically proceeded by rote memorization, and curiosity was often actively discouraged. Carroll's Alice books were, among other things, a Victorian satirist's gloss on the wrongheadedness of this and all forms of mindless authority. Tenniel in turn had nimbly advanced the theme by visualizing Wonderland as a fairground version of the intimidating obstacle course by means of which Victorian adults suppressed their children's natural inquisitiveness.

In contrast to all this, parents, teachers, and psychologists now took it for granted — in theory at any rate — that curiosity and imagination were developmental positives: a blessing, not a curse.

Facing page: From Alice Through the Looking-Glass, *Walker, 2005*

Pages 202–203: From Alice's Adventures in Wonderland, *Walker, 1999*

Maurice Sendak's *Where the Wild Things Are* — a picture book fable celebrating the power of imagination to serve the child's emotional well-being — had crystallized the post-Freudian view.

Alice, like Max, might be thought of as Every Child, her adventures a comically exaggerated reprise of the universal quest to learn, early on in life, the difference between reality and make-believe. To the girl in white tennis shoes, the journey through Wonderland was just one more strange and "curious" experience.

Alice gave Helen a grand stage on which to show off her complete repertoire as an illustrator. It called for satirical portraiture like the character drawings she had done decades earlier for *Cakes and Custard*; imaginary beasts like the ones for *The Quangle Wangle's Hat* and *The Dragon of an Ordinary Family*; naturalistic animals in human predicaments (some but not all in human dress) like those drawn for Eugene Trivizas's *The Three Little Wolves and the Big Bad Pig* and Martin Waddell's *Farmer Duck*. There were landscapes, domestic interiors, fantasy sequences involving playing cards come to life, and more.

Pages 204–205, facing page, and right:
From Alice Through the Looking-Glass, *Walker, 2005*

Helen decked out certain characters — the churlish Duchess, for example — not in contemporary or Victorian attire but rather in the soigné fashions of the 1920s, an era that fascinated her in part for having been the heyday of her parents' generation. For Helen, the story of Alice would forever be linked to the sound of her mother's voice reading aloud to her all those years earlier. The fashion mash-up also suited Carroll's maverick vision: *Alice*'s winking wit, and the acute mistrust the book proclaimed for all assumed orders and fixed ideas.

Published simultaneously in 1999 by Walker and Candlewick, *Alice's Adventures in Wonderland* was awarded that year's Kate Greenaway Medal, Helen's second. It had been a monumental undertaking, a kind of sprinter's marathon, with nearly one hundred drawings of differing sizes and degrees of complexity ultimately required. The project had taken far longer than planned, and, as absorbing as the work had been, Helen was not about to launch directly into the sequel. She turned instead to a manuscript that had come for her consideration from far-off Cambridge, Massachusetts, where Walker's thriving American outpost, Candlewick Press, was now generating projects of its own.

Facing page and right: From Alice's Adventures in Wonderland, *Walker, 1999*

2000S

Creation Story

The manuscript, by a Minnesota writer named Phyllis Root, was — of all things — a brassy retelling of the biblical creation story, called *Big Momma Makes the World*. This time, when Helen joined David Lloyd for their lunchtime courtship ritual, she pointedly went off script and ordered dessert before Lloyd could get around to the reading. One hearing of Root's audacious manuscript, in which the God of Genesis was recast as a single working mother with a baby to look after, turned out to be quite enough to win Helen's approval.

Big Momma was *Meal One* raised to a higher — celestial! — power. The writing was salty, vigorous, and big-spirited. It all but sang itself off the page.

For Helen, a few pangs of buyer's remorse were the predictable aftermath, as the enormity of the task she had agreed to undertake fully registered. It was one thing for an author to describe — in a few telegraphed words — the first flash of creation: "'Light,' said Big Momma. And you better believe there was light." It was quite another matter for an illustrator to visualize the scene in convincing detail.

Then, just as predictably, Helen rebounded in her customary way: by homing in on the human dimension, "concentrating on

Previous pages: Early sketches for Big Momma Makes the World, *c. 2001*
Facing page: From Big Momma Makes the World, *Candlewick, 2003*

the two characters, especially the baby, and simplifying the background right down to a scale I could manage, and which made it more accessible to young children."

She had once again looked for — and taken — the child's side. This, at least, was the half of it. Painted in luminous gouache, the illustrations celebrated babyhood, but they also paid tribute to a mother's love for her child, and they did so from both a personal and an archetypal perspective. Helen had in effect placed motherhood — so often a culturally marginalized role — at the very center of creation.

When *Big Momma Makes the World* won the 2003 Boston Globe–Horn Book Award, Helen returned to the United States to join Root at the ceremony. In unusually personal prepared remarks, she reflected on the challenges of illustrating the book. She noted that because Big Momma and her baby were both characters cast in human form, she had been compelled to consider the matter of their skin color and race — not a simple question under the circumstances: "I didn't want to, and indeed I couldn't, decide on any particular race or ethnic group." Finally, she told the audience, she had chosen to "let both of them take on the color of whatever Big Momma was creating at the time, so they became one with the water, or light, or mud, or grass."

Facing page and next pages: From Big Momma Makes the World, *Candlewick, 2003*   **215**

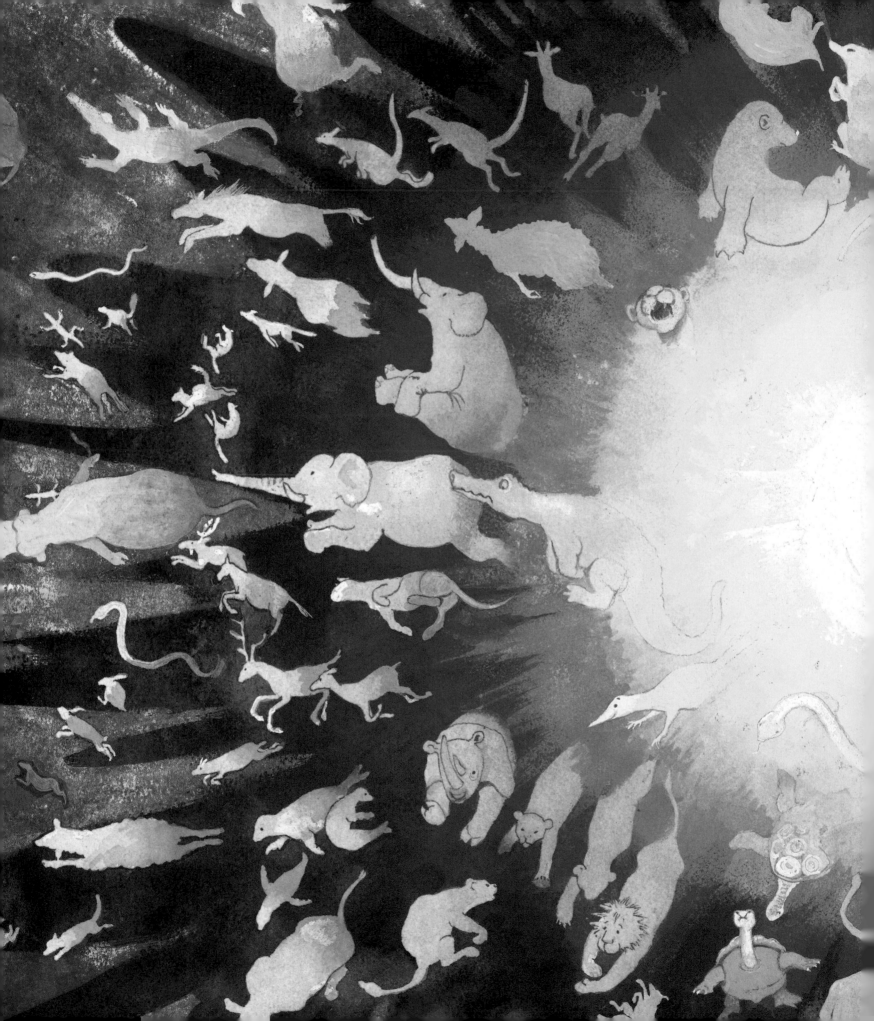

Illustrating the book had also stirred painful memories of her childhood years as a student in a convent school where it was taken for granted that God — "authoritative, judgmental, and dominating" — was male, and where she and her schoolmates had been "surrounded by horrific images of suffering and sadness." She contrasted the joyless experience of reciting the catechism by rote with the thrill of encountering Phyllis Root's robust, thought-provoking words.

Adult readers of *Big Momma* were bound to take Root's unorthodox portrayal of the Creator as a feminist declaration (all the more so in the case of those who recognized in Root's text strong echoes of Harlem Renaissance poet James Weldon Johnson's black-liberation narrative "The Creation"). In a letter to Candlewick editor Amy Ehrlich, Helen wrote that she would be glad for any "ruffled feathers" the book might occasion on that account.

"I see Big Momma as highlighting the complex condition of women," she explained. "It is impossibly hard for women today — so much is expected of them. They have the children, create the environment that they live in, nurture this environment, bring up their children, and, more than likely, hold down a responsible job to boot. And then they have to sparkle on a social level!" With an

From Big Momma Makes the World, *Candlewick, 2003*

affectionate nod to John Burningham, she added, "This is all easier with an enlightened partner, but so many women now — like Big Momma — have to cope single-handed. I don't know how they manage."

Magic Strings of Words

The globalization of children's book publishing opened the door wide for an artist of Helen's stature to collaborate with writers everywhere. By the turn of the new century, while the lion's share of her book projects continued to emanate from London, it was no great surprise when an American publisher, Houghton Mifflin Harcourt, proposed a collaboration between Helen and an Australian mainstay of the HMH list, picture book author Mem Fox. Anyone could see that this was an inspired pairing, not least on account of Fox's eloquent advocacy, in her parallel career as a literacy activist, of the very kinds of books for which Helen was famous.

The manuscript of *Ten Little Fingers and Ten Little Toes* was one of those deceptively simple read-alouds that packed a world of tender regard into its compact magic strings of words. It could be read or sung as a lullaby or lightly explored as a first counting book

From Big Momma Makes the World, *Candlewick, 2003*

or simply embraced as a chance for a playful parent and child to tickle and tease each other. Fox invited readers to consider — and her collaborator to draw — numbers of babies and toddlers of a variety of racial backgrounds and ethnicities and, in a spirit of hope, to view them all as having more in common with one another than not.

For Helen, *Ten Little Fingers and Ten Little Toes* represented a new opportunity to make expressive action drawings of small children and to experiment with landscape, composition, and color. In one striking, poster-like image of a mother and her baby, she chose, counterintuitively, to turn the red armchair in which the mother is sitting almost entirely away from the reader. The view allows for only the merest glimpse of the pair as they enjoy a peaceful, private moment together. Completely unmoored from its surroundings, the chair in this remarkable drawing floats in white space. It is as though the mother and child, huddled lovingly together in the chair's unseen depths, inhabit a world that is all their own — as in a very real way they do. Here is a drawing not just of people and their things, but of a core human relationship, an image that does not so much describe an experience as embody it. Here too is a classic Helen Oxenbury take on the koan-like injunction to

make art in which less is more, an ideal and an ambition shared by picture book innovators from Randolph Caldecott to Maurice Sendak.

Full Circle

Although John and Helen had occasionally come to each other's aid over the years with a helpful comment about work in progress, and although John had often become quite involved in Helen's books for younger readers as an uncredited writer and editor, the couple had never joined forces to create a full-dress picture book, when, early in 2010, advance word went out that *There's Going to Be a Baby* was about to be published, with text by John and illustrations by Helen. A first-ever collaboration so late in both their celebrated careers made a good story in itself, and press reports were soon furnishing critics and fans with details of the project's surprisingly long and winding prehistory.

Helen, it turned out, had made her first drawings for a version of the text ten years earlier but had been stopped cold by a difficulty for which neither she nor John could find a satisfactory remedy. The text fell naturally into two parts: bits of conversation between a mother and her child about the imminent arrival of a new baby in their family and, intermixed with these exchanges, scenes from the young child's fantasies about the baby's future life, several of them cast in wildly exaggerated terms meant to reflect the older child's emotional confusion. The fantasy element was intended to puncture the fears of children facing the same classic predicament while also giving both parent and child a good laugh.

From the outset, however, the nagging question for Helen had been how best to style the fantasy images in such a way as to distinguish them graphically from the scenes set in the present. As she recalled for an interviewer: "The early pictures were all of the baby dressed up for his future life: as a farmer, a lorry driver, a steeplejack, a this and a that. The problem was that the baby was too realistic and it looked grotesque. And for some reason we had decided not to have the mother in the illustrations at all. The breakthrough came when we realized that, yes, we must have the mum in the pictures along with her little son, and make the imaginary episodes of what the baby was going to do when he grew up a separate entity."

In the end, Helen found a suitable look for the child's imaginings in a retro drawing style inspired by *Beano*, a weekly comic that she and John had both grown up with, featuring waggish characters

From There's Going to Be a Baby, *Walker, 2010*

THERE'S GOING TO BE A BABY

JOHN BURNINGHAM & HELEN OXENBURY

like the McTickles family and Uncle Windbag. In her *Beano* reprise, Helen held true not only to the comic's panel-sequence format but also to the limited color palette of the originals (a consequence of the 1940s wartime rationing of inks and dyes) and even to the dot-screen pattern that was synonymous with the cheap color printing of bygone days. The contrasting reality-based illustrations of the mother and child each occupied a full page, with scenes of the pair out and about at a coffeehouse, an art museum, a bank, and elsewhere.

"The story," Helen recalled, "was purely about the relationship between two strong characters. For that reason it needed simplicity and within that simplicity, the most important thing was to focus on the expressions of the mother and the little boy."

Simple the drawings may have been, but Helen had achieved that end by a subtle blending of graphic elements, balancing the primacy of line against that of color, pictorial narrative against abstract form. In so doing, she arrived at the practiced casualness of Japanese

Facing page, right, and next pages:
From There's Going to Be a Baby, *Walker, 2010*

woodblock prints. In the name of realism, she had made a running joke over the years of the tired, haggard mothers who scrambled from scene to scene coping with family life's rude little surprises. Here, in contrast, Helen dressed the pregnant mother in smart clothes and gave her a poised and confident expression.

She had, it seemed, taken this occasion to remind young mothers that, all joking aside, a strong sense of self was a good and viable option. Now a grandmother, Helen had come to feel a motherly concern as much for the mothers in her books as for their children. The circle of the story she had to tell had grown larger with time.

Left, facing page, and next pages:
From There's Going to Be a Baby, *Walker, 2010*

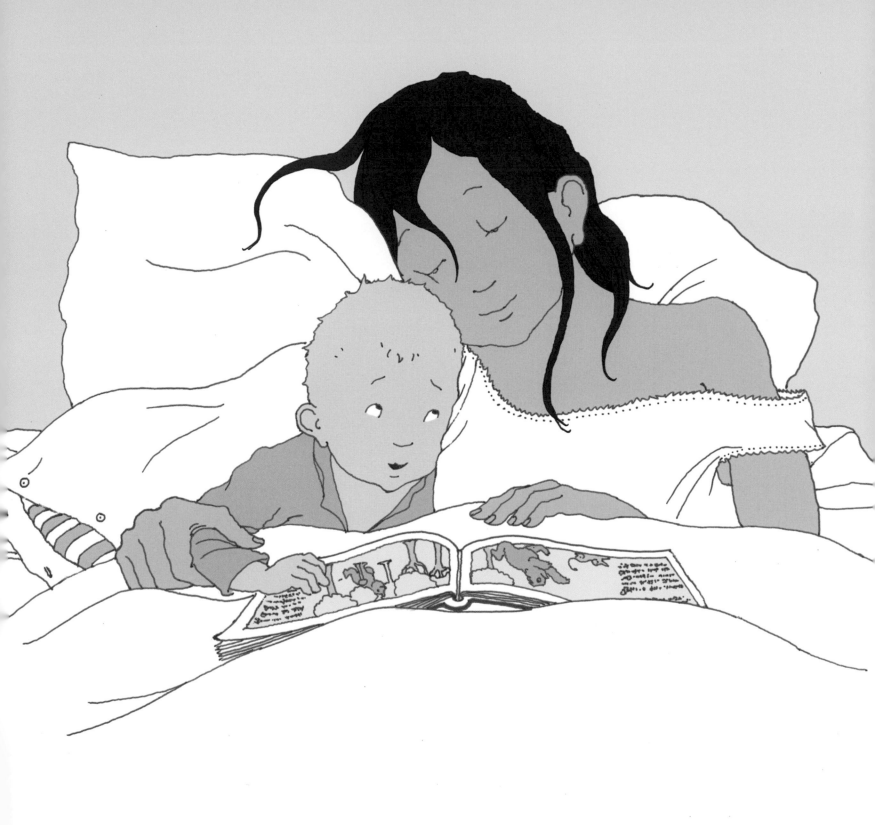

Luminous Space

To a keen observer like Helen, places were bound to matter as much as people. One place that has mattered a great deal to her is Felixstowe Ferry, the fishing hamlet and summer resort on the Deben Estuary, in Suffolk, East Anglia, near the town of Felixstowe, where as a child she passed many happy, active years.

Helen's parents stayed on in the traditional coastal town long after their daughter had left for London, but even after Bernard and Muriel Oxenbury came to live next door to the Burninghams in London, Helen continued to feel the pull of the Suffolk seaside and to return there often, finally as the owner of a wooden boathouse turned weekend getaway with a panoramic waterside view.

Long before Bill Burningham helped them restore the wobbly structure, John and Helen had gone to town fitting it out with offbeat finds from their regular jumble shop foragings: here a massive tarpon mounted in a glass case, there a battered steamer trunk and bright display of Delft tiles. Fading vintage photos of the working boathouse and its denizens hung in the front room, while framed on the bathroom wall were

Previous pages: From We're Going on a Bear Hunt, *Walker, 1989*
Right and facing page: One of Helen's clay sculptures, a boy and his hen, c. 1998

244

wilting lyrics by the sentimental songstress Patience Strong. A circular wooden staircase salvaged from an old church spiraled up to an added-on second-story aerie. For all that it contained, the little house felt cozy, not cramped, with the tall riverside windows well positioned to induce the pleasurable sensation in occupants of being out on the water rather than merely beside it. Boathouse . . . houseboat . . . it was a daydreamy, out-of-time, far-from-anywhere kind of place: a two-hour drive and a world away from London. If there was a drawing table in the house, it was not left out for a visitor to see.

In late November 2013, Helen, John, David Lloyd, and I, having met up a few days earlier in London, piled into a car and threaded our way northeast to Suffolk. I had come along to work on a book — this book — about Helen. The plan was to spend a quiet weekend in her home territory as, Boswell-like, I absorbed the atmosphere of the place, posed the occasional question, and otherwise gathered "material."

Tall reeds edged the bumpy, narrow last long stretch of road that ended at a padlocked chain-link gate. Just beyond this lay the boathouse and a huddle of low-slung cottages and sheds.

The Suffolk air had turned bitterly cold, and as we regrouped indoors around the kitchen table over hot coffee, Helen was in a reflective mood. It was not just that she — ever the intensely private person — was now to be the subject of a book. On the calendar for 2014 were the festivities — and inevitable rounds of press interviews and "appearances" — that would surround *We're Going on a Bear Hunt*'s twenty-fifth anniversary.

Also in the offing was a group exhibition at the Ipswich Art School Gallery in which examples of her illustration art would hang beside work by other children's book artists who had grown up in East Anglia, or studied there, or drawn inspiration from the region.

All in all, it was an impressive roster. Helen's contemporaries Michael Foreman and John Lawrence were to be represented in the show, as were the once wildly popular Johnstone twins (recalled most often now as the illustrators of Dodie Smith's *The Hundred and One Dalmatians*),

Left: Helen's clay sculpture of a boy, c. 1998
Facing page: Helen's clay sculpture of a dog, c. 1998

and one of Helen's illustration idols, Edward Ardizzone. Ardizzone's maternal grandmother had raised him from early boyhood in Ipswich at the turn of the last century, and he had gone on to attend the same school at which Helen received her foundational training. Yet the perennially marginalized status of illustration within the art world at large had done little over the years to build a sense of communal tradition in the ranks of East Anglia's illustrators. For many who eventually viewed the show, Helen among them, the exhibition would come as a revelation.

"A seaside town in the summer is magical," Helen observed of her carefree early years there. (The name Felixstowe is formed of the Latin and Anglo-Saxon root words for "happy" or "blessed" and "place.") "But in the winter a seaside town is pretty dead."

All the same, I thought, as the chill air easily bored its way through four layers of clothes, a remote place like this was well situated to offer escape from the myriad distractions of career and city. John liked nothing better than to disappear for an hour or more into a hard-fought round of Scrabble. ("Is xi a word?" he could be heard gamely growling from the

next room.) Helen preferred leisurely walks with her Jack Russell, Myles, on the footpath along the river wall.

The morning after our arrival, I accompanied Helen on the day's first outing. We soon came to a gaily decked-out houseboat moored in the mudflats and, just beyond it, two abandoned wooden hulls that appeared almost to be posing for their pictures. In the early light at low tide the stretch of mud on the far side of the river wall looked to have been sculpted satiny-smooth. The oozy, raw, primordial expanse was an adventurous child's paradise: we had arrived in *Bear Hunt* country.

With no hills or mountains in sight, the sky, clouded over that morning almost to the horizon, dominated the view as it cast its silvery-gray light in every direction. I found myself recalling the luminous white space in so many of Helen's drawings. Had I now come face-to-face with its source? This question was not one, I realized, that could be easily answered. Artists, I knew, had often commented about the region's distinctive light, which had galvanized (among others) the Romantic landscape painter John Constable and, several decades later, the English impressionist painters of nearby Walberswick. What about Helen, though?

"The light here is special," she said back at the boathouse. "It

Helen's clay sculpture of a lady reclining in a deck chair, c. 2017

often is, along the coast — certainly compared with London. It's the clarity of the atmosphere. *Bear Hunt*," Helen went on, "cried out to be illustrated in watercolor in part because it is about the light."

This last thought had not occurred to me, and it went a long way toward explaining the feeling of dramatic immediacy — of "being there" — that comes through so strongly in Helen's art.

New picture books appear by the thousand each year; all but a few quickly come and go. A book can become a cherished presence in a child's, or family's, life — or not. That Helen Oxenbury's books have made such a lasting impression for such a good long time now is an achievement worth celebrating in all its dimensions. Here is drawing and watercolor art in the classic English tradition and of a very high standard. Here is a lightly held but deeply felt — and considered — view of childhood, parenting, and family relations. Here in simple-seeming words and pictures are fundamental tales of what it means to be new to the world, and not quite new, and, above all, human.

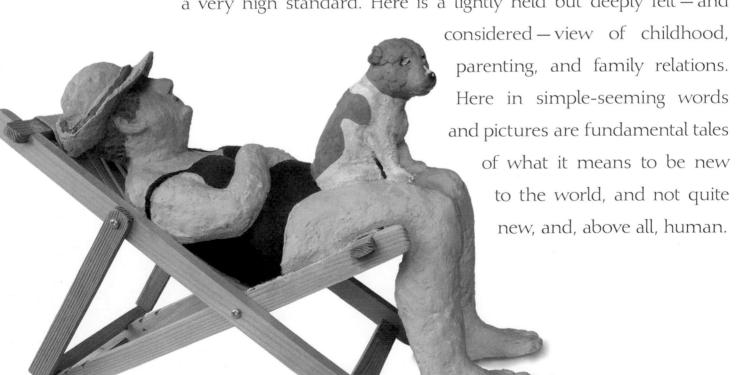

Postscripts

TRISH COOKE

HELEN'S BOARD BOOKS, the Tom and Pippo series, and books such as We're Going on a Bear Hunt *and* Farmer Duck *were already firm favorites with my son Kieron when I heard that Helen Oxenbury would be illustrating* So Much. *I loved her work and felt very excited. Although I didn't meet Helen until after the book had been completed, I think it is fair to say that, after many drafts, once Mara and David (the editors) and Amelia (the art director) agreed that it was finished, I didn't need to meet her, as the final text spoke for itself and Helen was able to have fun with it in a manner only she knows how.*

I think the thing that amazed me most about Helen's illustrations was the way, somehow, she managed to spirit herself into my head and share the memories that I have with my family and transfer the images onto the pages of the book as if she had lived it, been there. She never saw any photographs of my family, and yet she was able to capture the essence of them within her vibrant, colorful illustrations. Some of the characters even look like family members, which is spooky, and afterward when I went through my album I even found photographs of my family that mirrored the poses that Helen had drawn. When you come across an artist as in tune with your work as that, it is impossible to feel anything other than admiration.

Having Helen Oxenbury illustrate So Much *was a truly magical experience.*

Previous pages: Helen and John at their Suffolk boathouse, c. 1987
Above: Trish Cooke
Facing page: From So Much, *Walker, 1994*

MEM FOX

I DON'T KNOW WHERE I was when my American editor, Allyn Johnston, suggested Helen Oxenbury as a possible illustrator for Ten Little Fingers and Ten Little Toes, *but I do recall thinking what a pie-in-the-sky idea it was. Helen? My book? As if she'd ever agree to that! Secretly, I thought I might fall senseless to the floor if she said yes, as I'd been such a worshipful fan for so many years.*

I received the good news while I was on holiday on remote Lord Howe Island. It came by fax from America. Even then faxes were becoming dated, but it was particularly wonderful to have that waxy piece of paper to wave around and dance with. Everyone in the hotel knew about it. And then, months later, the pictures came. Oh, the lump in my throat! Wherever one goes, as everyone knows, Helen's babies are the most adorable in the world and so funny. Their every look, gesture, and posture are so true they seem to giggle back at you from the page. I was over the moon, reeling from my luck.

But much better was to come. Helen and I were asked to do a book tour together in the U.S.A. I was hideously nervous about meeting her. I knew I would babble incoherently, like one of the babies in the book. She was typically English: dignified, stately, contained. I was typically Australian, once I'd got over my awe: untrammeled, effusive, overwhelming. It shouldn't have worked, but it did — like magic. We had such fun together, pricking each other's bubbles in comic fashion as we talked about our book in many different public places.

Above: Mem Fox
Facing page: From Ten Little Fingers and Ten Little Toes, *Walker, 2008*

I fell in love with her, and on our last morning, as we were parting, she said in her divinely English manner, "You're all right, after all!"

Ten Little Fingers and Ten Little Toes was Australia's official gift to Prince George on his birth in 2013. Hmm. It must be all right, after all!

PHYLLIS ROOT

I HAVE TRIED AND TRIED to say what I want to say about Helen. She is beyond words. She is amazing. My children and I loved her books for babies when they were babies, and I have admired and looked for her work ever since.

Having Helen do the art for Big Momma Makes the World was a gift unlooked-for, life altering. Big Momma's bra in the laundry picture made me laugh, and the animals and little baby comforting a lonely Big Momma made me cry. I want to live in the world she created. I want to lie down in the picture of the hammock and eat the papayas and oranges and mangoes with that little baby of hers. I want to eat her biscuits and listen to the stories of the folks she made so she wouldn't be lonely.

Meeting Helen in London for the book launch, seeing her art projected on the ceiling of the London Planetarium while the book was read, watching the children present wave their balloon swords in time to the London Gospel Choir singing, was one of the great gifts of my writing life.

Helen's art is beautiful, humorous, joyful, generous, just as Helen is. Like Big Momma, Helen creates worlds, and that's good. That's real good.

258

Above: Phyllis Root
Facing page: From Big Momma Makes the World, *Candlewick, 2003*

MICHAEL ROSEN

I HAVE ALREADY CONFESSED this several times before, but I don't mind confessing it again. When I first saw the pictures that Helen did for Bear Hunt I couldn't "read" them; I didn't "get" them. I had sent Walker Books my adaptation of the traditional chant "We're Going on a Bear Hunt" with my own absurd ideas for what such a book might look like. Some two years later I was invited in to see Helen's work. Editors and designers ushered me to a darkened room where a pile of large sheets of handmade paper lay on a table. Each sheet was itself covered in a thin sheet of colored paper.

They peeled back the colored sheets and revealed each of Helen's paintings one by one. As they peeled they sighed and turned to me, trying to read my face for reactions.

Now the confession: I looked and looked, but I couldn't see. What I thought I saw was a set of pictures telling the story of a family group on holiday in somewhere like Cornwall or Norfolk on the English coast. But why? I asked myself. There aren't any bears on the Cornish or Norfolk coast in England.

I said that I liked the pictures — I did. One or two of them reminded me of Renoir, others of Constable. But what is it about, what is it all for? I could see and hear that the professionals in the room thought that this was something extra-special. But why? Why did they think that? I couldn't figure it.

Then the book came out. And there was an explosion. People seemed to compete with each other to say why and how it was such a brilliant book. I still didn't get it.

Above: Michael Rosen
Facing page: From We're Going on a Bear Hunt, *Walker, 1989*

O fool! O insensitive log!

After listening to children and adults who've shared the book with children, and having done so myself too, I now "get" what others got right from the start. Helen took the words and created a new story, a story that is not told in the words, a story about a family grouping struggling — we know not why — with the elements that the world throws at us. While the adult reading the story provides what musicians call "the groove," the stories provide the melody — the soulful, spiritual journey that we all go on: facing up to difficulties, overcoming them, and struggling to get home. Each of Helen's great paintings show the struggle being faced by each individual in the family grouping but also as they assist and cooperate with one another in lines of empathy that reach across each page and out to the readers and lookers-on of the book.

Each figure, each part of the landscape, and each whole composition offers us feelings. The shape of the figures, the color of the sky, the movement across the pages and between the pages enable everyone from the very youngest of children to interpret this drama for themselves. And this is all invented and created by Helen. And it prioritizes the child looker-on, because in most circumstances, the wordy stuff is read out loud by the adult and the child is left to probe and question Helen's paintings.

As it happens, the traditional chant offers a surging, repetitive, rhythmic framework that most children know almost before they know it. But the depth and emotional body of the book come from Helen's pictures.

I will forever be in debt, first to David Lloyd, who spotted me performing the chant and said that it would make a good children's book, and second to Helen, for creating this wonderful chain of images, and finally to Amelia, who, with Helen, designed the book.

From We're Going on a Bear Hunt, *Walker, 1989*

MARTIN WADDELL

FOR ME, THE REAL MAGIC of Helen's Farmer Duck lies in the world she creates for him. On the front cover, a lonely duck hoeing in a plowed field. How does a duck hold a hoe? Only Helen knows! Open the book, wider shot of the field, misty cold, no sign of the duck-all-alone. Title page, the duck waddling back to the farm, where the other animals wait. Interior of the farmer's bedroom, beer and chocolate and he wears a cap in bed, whilst the duck fetches him an ice cream; labors of Hercules, then a reprise of the fat farmer munching his chocolates: the image that children love best in the book. More labors, funny and varied, then the hinge illustration that turns the story: "The poor duck was sleepy and weepy and tired." The collapsed duck surrounded by hen friends . . . that's a great story-telling body-language picture. . . . Look at the hen who nestles against the duck's feathers. Look at the splayed feet of the exhausted duck. The moo-baa-clucking conspiracy leading to the moo-baa-cluck overthrow of the farmer, his cap flying off his head, followed by his flight through the fields and the relief of "And he never came back." From that point on, the sun and the duck both shine, leading to the endpaper, where the dismal fields at the beginning of the book are replaced by gold and green and sunlight as we leave their farm.

I love Helen's illustrations for their vigor, imagination, powerful storytelling . . . and sheer fun. I love the duck, Helen's duck, my duck, our duck.

I'm sure George Orwell would too.

Above: Martin Waddell
Facing page: From Farmer Duck, *Walker, 1991*
Next pages: From Time Now to Dream, *Walker, 2016*

Bibliography

U.S. publisher noted in parentheses.

1967 Numbers of Things

Heinemann (Delacorte) *See pages 54–57*

1968 The Great Big Enormous Turnip

By Alexei Tolstoy; translated by E. Schinanskaya

Heinemann (Franklin Watts) *See pages 57–59*

1969 The Dragon of an Ordinary Family

By Margaret Mahy

Heinemann (Dial) *See pages 62–67*

The Quangle Wangle's Hat

By Edward Lear

Heinemann *See pages 62–65*

Letters of Thanks

By Manghanita Kempadoo

Collins

1970 The Hunting of the Snark

By Lewis Carroll

Heinemann

1971 Meal One

By Ivor Cutler

Heinemann (Franklin Watts) *See pages 71–77*

Helen Oxenbury's ABC of Things

Heinemann (Delacorte)

268

1973 Pig Tale

Heinemann (Margaret K. McElderry Books)

1974 Cakes and Custard

Edited by Brian Alderson

Heinemann (William Morrow) *See pages 78–83*

1975 Balooky Klujypop

By Ivor Cutler

Heinemann

1976 The Animal House

By Ivor Cutler

Heinemann (William Morrow)

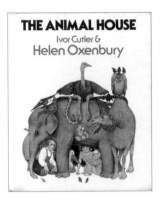

1978 The Queen and Rosie Randall

From an idea by Jill Buttfield-Campbell

Heinemann (William Morrow)

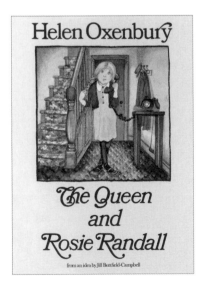

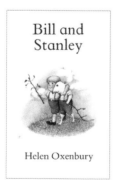

1984 Gran and Grandpa
Our Dog
The Visitor

Walker See pages 106–117

1985 I Can
I Hear
I See
I Touch

*first published exclusively for
J Sainsbury plc*

Walker (Candlewick) *See pages 100–101*

The Helen Oxenbury
Nursery Story Book

Heinemann (Knopf)

1986 The Helen Oxenbury
Nursery Rhyme Book

Edited by Brian Alderson

Heinemann (William Morrow)

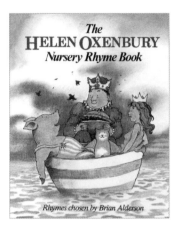

1987 All Fall Down
Clap Hands
Say Goodnight
Tickle, Tickle

Walker (Margaret K. McElderry
Books) *See pages 120–131*

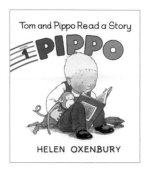

Tom and Pippo Read a Story

HELEN OXENBURY

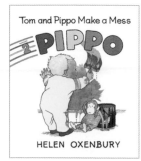

Tom and Pippo Make a Mess

HELEN OXENBURY

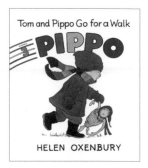

Tom and Pippo Go for a Walk

HELEN OXENBURY

Tom and Pippo and the Washing Machine

HELEN OXENBURY

Tom and Pippo Go Shopping

HELEN OXENBURY

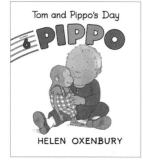

Tom and Pippo's Day

HELEN OXENBURY

Tom and Pippo in the Garden

HELEN OXENBURY

Tom and Pippo See the Moon

HELEN OXENBURY

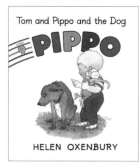

Tom and Pippo and the Dog

HELEN OXENBURY

Tom and Pippo in the Snow

HELEN OXENBURY

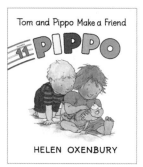

Tom and Pippo Make a Friend

HELEN OXENBURY

Pippo Gets Lost

HELEN OXENBURY

1989

Tom and Pippo
and the Dog

Tom and Pippo
in the Snow

Tom and Pippo
Make a Friend

Pippo Gets Lost

Walker (Aladdin)

1991

Farmer Duck

By Martin Waddell
Walker (Candlewick) *See pages 156–170, 264–265*

The Helen Oxenbury Nursery Treasury

Edited by Brian Alderson
Heinemann

1992

Tom and Pippo
on the Beach

*first published exclusively
for J Sainsbury plc*
Walker

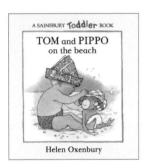

1993

The Three Little Wolves
and the Big Bad Pig

By Eugene Trivizas
Heinemann (Margaret K. McElderry
Books) *See pages 132–133, 172–177*

Tom and Pippo and
the Bicycle

*first published exclusively
for J Sainsbury plc*
Walker

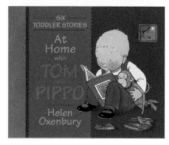
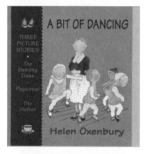

2001

Franny B. Kranny, There's a Bird in Your Hair!

By Harriet Lerner and Susan Goldhor

Walker (HarperCollins)

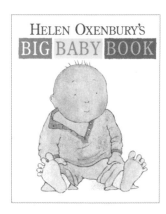

2002

Helen Oxenbury's Big Baby Book

Walker (Candlewick)

Big Mama Makes the World

By Phyllis Root

Walker (Candlewick) *See pages 210–221, 258–259*

2003

The Helen Oxenbury Nursery Collection

Egmont

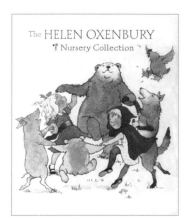

2005

Alice Through the Looking-Glass

By Lewis Carroll

Walker (Candlewick) *See pages 18, 20–21, 201–207*

2007

The Growing Story

By Ruth Krauss

HarperCollins (HarperCollins)

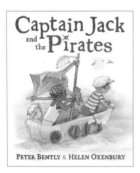
Facing page: From Charley's First Night, *Walker, 2012*
Next pages: From The Giant Jumperee, *Puffin, 2017*

ACKNOWLEDGMENTS

I wish to express my thanks to the following individuals who agreed to be interviewed for this book, or who made available needed source materials in their possession or care: Liz Attenborough, Brett Brubaker, Allison Bruce, Joanna Carey, Justin Chandra, Susan Cooper Cronyn, Donald Davis, Mary Lee Donovan, Emma Dryden, Amy Ehrlich, Judith M. Elliott, David Ford, Sarah Foster, Sharon Hancock, Irina Klyagin, Marilyn Malin, James Mayhew, Annie Nybo, Michelle Pauli, Jan Pieńkowski, Neal Porter, Emma Roodhouse, Deborah Sloan, Georgina Tibbott, Judy Willcocks, and Liz Wood.

Thanks too to Trish Cooke, Mem Fox, Phyllis Root, Michael Rosen, and Martin Waddell for their thoughtful commentaries, newly written for this book, about Helen's pictures for their words.

I am grateful to my late agent George M. Nicholson of Sterling Lord Literistic for his clear-eyed guidance through the publishing maze and for his eagerness to share his broad knowledge of British publishing.

It has been a pleasure to work with the staffs of Walker Books and Candlewick Press. I thank Karen Lotz and Deirdre McDermott for entrusting me with this project, and Deirdre and Andrea Aboagye as well for completing the last stages of the book's complex design. I thank my editors David Lloyd and Lizzie Sitton for the great skill with which they shaped the manuscript and succeeded in bringing this big book's many component parts into harmonious alignment. Additional thanks to David for the patience and high humor with which he recalled Walker's beginnings for my benefit, and to the late Amelia Edwards for her splendid design work and for the time she graciously spent with me while recounting Walker's formative years. Back in New York, Candlewick's Sarah Ketchersid was a delight to work with as we prepared the American edition together.

Sadly, Helen's capable archivist Louise Power did not live to see the completion of this book. I benefited substantially not only from her detailed responses to my queries about artwork and publication histories but also from her unwavering good cheer. I thank Perry Emerson for carrying forward the work of retrieving and scanning art needed for the book and for clearing needed permissions.

Finally, a most heartfelt thank-you to John Burningham and Emily Burningham for their friendship and encouragement, and to Helen Oxenbury for the forthrightness and grace with which she told her story to me and allowed me into her world.

Leonard S. Marcus
New York, 2018

THE WALKER BEAR

In the very earliest of Walker days, Sebastian Walker, along with founding art director Amelia Edwards, asked Helen to draw the logo for his fledgling company. This probably happened in the office right at the top of the rickety stairs on Drummond Street, central London; the date for the logo's genesis, hard to remember now, is most likely around 1985. Helen initially drew the bear in fine black line, soon afterward reimagining it in assured pencil and effortless watercolor.

The Walker Bear is always in motion, right foot first, perpetually carrying the flickering candle in its green candlestick — respected the world over as a symbol of publishing quality and distinction. That confident and happy brown bear, with the warm glow of a bright candle's flame on its nose and tummy, has made a mark, literally, on every single book that we publish.

So it is that the story of Helen Oxenbury's astonishing contribution to children's books is intrinsically woven into the fabric and legacy of Walker Books and Candlewick Press. She is as steeped in our history as we are in hers. Helen's beautiful, iconic bear has illuminated the creative path for the thousands of stories that we've published, and shines a way forward for the many, many more to come.

Deirdre McDermott
Publisher, Walker Books
London, 2018

SIGNIFICANT AWARDS

1969   Kate Greenaway Medal for *The Dragon of an Ordinary Family* and *The Quangle Wangle's Hat*

1989   Nestlé Smarties Book Prize for *We're Going on a Bear Hunt*

1991   Nestlé Smarties Book Prize for *Farmer Duck*

1991   Children's Book of the Year at the British Book Awards for *Farmer Duck*

1994   Kurt Maschler Award for *So Much*

1994   Nestlé Smarties Book Prize for *So Much*

1999   Kurt Maschler Award for *Alice's Adventures in Wonderland*

1999   Kate Greenaway Medal for *Alice's Adventures in Wonderland*

1999   BookTrust Early Years Award for *Tickle, Tickle*

2003   *Boston Globe–Horn Book* Award for *Big Momma Makes the World*

2015   Eric Carle Artist Honor

2018   BookTrust Lifetime Achievement Award

From Tom and Pippo Read a Story, *Walker, 1988*

PERMISSIONS & CREDITS

PAGES 1, 2–3, 10–16 — Photographs of Helen and her studio © 2018 Nobby Clark/Arena PAL and used with permission

PAGES 4, 5, 8, 9 — From *Alice's Adventures in Wonderland*, Walker, 1999

PAGE 7 — From *It's My Birthday*, Walker, 1994

PAGE 54 — *Vegetable Garden* © Gallery Five, 1980, Series 03.08

PAGES 56–57 — Illustrations from *Numbers of Things* by Helen Oxenbury. Illustrations copyright © 1967 Helen Oxenbury. Published by Egmont UK Limited and used with permission

PAGES 58–59 — Illustration from *The Great Big Enormous Turnip* by Alexei Tolstoy, illustrated by Helen Oxenbury. Illustration copyright © 1968 Helen Oxenbury. Published by Egmont UK Limited and used with permission

PAGES 66–67 — Illustration from *The Dragon of an Ordinary Family* by Margaret Mahy, illustrated by Helen Oxenbury. Illustration copyright © 1969 Helen Oxenbury. Published by Egmont UK Limited and used with permission

PAGE 71 — Photograph of Ivor Cutler © Jeremy Cutler and used with permission

PAGE 118 — Photograph of Helen drawing with her daughter Emily by Gary Weaser for the *Guardian*

PAGES 173–177 — Illustrations from *The Three Little Wolves and the Big Bad Pig* by Eugene Trivizas, illustrated by Helen Oxenbury. Illustrations copyright © 1993 Helen Oxenbury. Published by Egmont UK Limited and used with permission

PAGES 222–230, 257 — Illustrations from *Ten Little Fingers* and *Ten Little Toes* by Mem Fox, illustrated by Helen Oxenbury. Illustrations copyright © 2008 by Helen Oxenbury. Reprinted by permission of Houghton Mifflin Harcourt Publishing Company. All rights reserved

PAGES 244–249 — Photographs of Helen's clay models © Michèle Clément-Delbos and used with permission

PAGES 250–251 — Photograph of Felixstowe mudflats © Leonard S. Marcus

PAGE 254 — Photograph of Trish Cooke © Kieron Ramsden

PAGE 268 — *Letters of Thanks* cover image reprinted by permission of HarperCollins Publishers Ltd © 1969 Manghanita Kempadoo and Helen Oxenbury

PAGE 270 — *Bill and Stanley* cover image, Ernest Benn Ltd, used by permission of Bloomsbury Publishing Plc

PAGE 275 — *The Growing Story* cover image reprinted by permission of HarperCollins Publishers Ltd © 2007 Ruth Krauss and Helen Oxenbury

PAGE 276 — Cover image reproduced from *King Jack and the Dragon* written by Peter Bently and illustrated by Helen Oxenbury (Puffin). With permission from Penguin Books Ltd. Copyright © 2011 Helen Oxenbury

PAGE 276 — Cover image reproduced from *Captain Jack and the Pirates* written by Peter Bently and illustrated by Helen Oxenbury (Puffin). With permission from Penguin Books Ltd. Copyright © 2015 Helen Oxenbury

PAGES 278–281 — Reproduced from *The Giant Jumperee* written by Julia Donaldson and illustrated by Helen Oxenbury (Puffin). With permission from Penguin Books Ltd. Copyright © 2017 Helen Oxenbury

PAGE 283 — From *Alice Through the Looking-Glass*, Walker, 2005